# NANCY'S FAVORITE
# 101 NOTIONS

## sew, quilt and embroider with ease

# NANCY ZIEMAN

KRAUSE PUBLICATIONS
CINCINNATI, OHIO

www.fwmedia.com

14  13  12  11  10    5  4  3  2  1

DISTRIBUTED IN CANADA BY FRASER DIRECT
100 Armstrong Avenue
Georgetown, ON, Canada  L7G 5S4
Tel:  (905) 877-4411

DISTRIBUTED IN THE U.K. AND EUROPE BY DAVID & CHARLES
Brunel House, Newton Abbot, Devon, TQ12 4PU, England
Tel: (+44) 1626 323200, Fax: (+44) 1626 323319
Email: postmaster@davidandcharles.co.uk

DISTRIBUTED IN AUSTRALIA BY CAPRICORN LINK
P.O. Box 704, S. Windsor NSW, 2756 Australia
Tel:  (02) 4577-3555

**Library of Congress Cataloging in Publication Data**
Zieman, Nancy Luedtke.
  Nancy's favorite 101 notions : sew, quilt, and embroider with ease / Nancy Zieman.
     p. cm.
  Includes index.
  ISBN-13: 978-0-89689-959-9 (pbk. : alk. paper)
  ISBN-10: 0-89689-959-4 (pbk. : alk. paper)
  1.  Needlework.  I. Title. II. Title: Favorite 101 notions.
  TT705.Z542 2010
  746.4--dc22
                                    2010014351

Edited by *Diane Dhein, Pat Hahn* and *Vanessa Lyman*

Designed by *Julie Barnett*

Production coordinated by *Greg Nock*

Illustrated by *Kristi C. Smith of Juicebox Designs*

| to convert | to | multiply by |
|---|---|---|
| inches | centimeters | 2.54 |
| centimeters | inches | 0.4 |
| feet | centimeters | 30.5 |
| centimeters | feet | 0.03 |
| yards | meters | 0.9 |
| meters | yards | 1.1 |

METRIC CONVERSION CHART

120"

## ABOUT THE AUTHOR

Nancy Zieman is executive producer and host of Public TV's *Sewing With Nancy*. She is also founder of Nancy's Notions, a direct mail company. In addition, she is an author and pattern and product designer.

She was named the 1988 Entrepreneurial Woman of the Year by the Wisconsin Women Entrepreneurs Association. In 1991, she received the National 4-H Alumni Award.

Nancy lives in Beaver Dam, Wisconsin, with her family.

## acknowledgments

To my friends and co-workers at Nancy's Notions who helped make my name synonymous with the word "notions." Thank you!

# CONTENTS

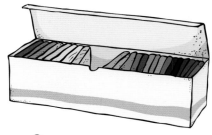

**Chapter 1**

## Gotta-Have Notions

**1** Marking Pens. . . . . . . . . . . . . . . . . . . . . . . . . . . 8
**2** Chalk. . . . . . . . . . . . . . . . . . . . . . . . . . . . . . . . . . 9
**3** Tracing Wheels and Tracing Paper . . . . . . . . . . . .10
**4** Sewing-Machine Seam Guides. . . . . . . . . . . . . . .12
**5** Pattern Weights . . . . . . . . . . . . . . . . . . . . . . . . .13
**6** Pincushions . . . . . . . . . . . . . . . . . . . . . . . . . . . .14
**7** Seam Rippers . . . . . . . . . . . . . . . . . . . . . . . . . . .15
**8** Pins . . . . . . . . . . . . . . . . . . . . . . . . . . . . . . . . . .16
**9** Buttonhole Cutters. . . . . . . . . . . . . . . . . . . . . . .18
**10** Thimbles. . . . . . . . . . . . . . . . . . . . . . . . . . . . . . .19
**11** Seam Gauges . . . . . . . . . . . . . . . . . . . . . . . . . . .20
**12** Tape Measures . . . . . . . . . . . . . . . . . . . . . . . . . .21
**13** Handsewing Needle Threaders . . . . . . . . . . . . . .22
**14** Machine Needle Inserter/Threaders . . . . . . . . . .24
**15** Needle-Gripping Tools. . . . . . . . . . . . . . . . . . . . .25
**16** Shears/Scissors . . . . . . . . . . . . . . . . . . . . . . . . . .26
**17** Awls/Stilettos . . . . . . . . . . . . . . . . . . . . . . . . . . .28
**18** Bodkins . . . . . . . . . . . . . . . . . . . . . . . . . . . . . . . .29

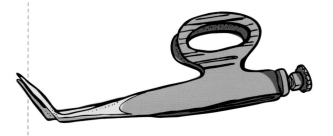

**Chapter 2**

## Get Organized

**19** Floor and Tabletop Task Lighting . . . . . . . . . . . . .32
**20** Sewing-Machine/Serger Task Lighting . . . . . . . .33
**21** Vacuum Attachments. . . . . . . . . . . . . . . . . . . . . .33
**22** Fabric Storage . . . . . . . . . . . . . . . . . . . . . . . . . . .34
**23** Ruler Storage . . . . . . . . . . . . . . . . . . . . . . . . . . .36
**24** Bobbin Organizers. . . . . . . . . . . . . . . . . . . . . . . .37
**25** Pattern Organizers. . . . . . . . . . . . . . . . . . . . . . . .38
**26** Thread Organizers . . . . . . . . . . . . . . . . . . . . . . . .39
**27** Trolley Organizers. . . . . . . . . . . . . . . . . . . . . . . .40
**28** Tote/Bag Organizers . . . . . . . . . . . . . . . . . . . . . .41

**Chapter 3**

## Just for Quilting

**29** Rotary Cutters . . . . . . . . . . . . . . . . . . . . . . . . . . .44
**30** Rotary-Blade Care Products . . . . . . . . . . . . . . . . .45
**31** Rulers. . . . . . . . . . . . . . . . . . . . . . . . . . . . . . . . . .46
**32** Marking Tape for Rulers . . . . . . . . . . . . . . . . . . . .47
**33** Ruler Gripper Handles . . . . . . . . . . . . . . . . . . . . .48
**34** Cutting Mats. . . . . . . . . . . . . . . . . . . . . . . . . . . .48
**35** Half-Square Triangle Helpers . . . . . . . . . . . . . . . .50
**36** On-Point Triangle Tools . . . . . . . . . . . . . . . . . . . .51
**37** Block Marking Rulers. . . . . . . . . . . . . . . . . . . . . .52
**38** Design Walls . . . . . . . . . . . . . . . . . . . . . . . . . . . .53
**39** Quarter-Inch Marking Tools . . . . . . . . . . . . . . . . .54
**40** Stencil Marking Tools . . . . . . . . . . . . . . . . . . . . .54
**41** Circle Cutting Aids . . . . . . . . . . . . . . . . . . . . . . . .55
**42** Binding Duo . . . . . . . . . . . . . . . . . . . . . . . . . . . .56
**43** Quilt Layering Tools . . . . . . . . . . . . . . . . . . . . . . .57
**44** Stippling/Meandering Notions . . . . . . . . . . . . . .58

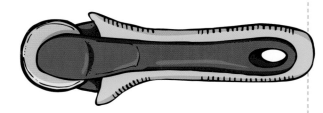

**Chapter 4**

## Thread-Tale Tools

**45** Thread Guides . . . . . . . . . . . . . . . . . . . . . . . . . . .62
**46** Thread Organizers . . . . . . . . . . . . . . . . . . . . . . . .63
**47** Thread Conditioners . . . . . . . . . . . . . . . . . . . . . .64
**48** Embroidery Clippers . . . . . . . . . . . . . . . . . . . . . .64
**49** Thread Removers . . . . . . . . . . . . . . . . . . . . . . . . .66
**50** Thread Braids . . . . . . . . . . . . . . . . . . . . . . . . . . . .67
**51** Needle Holders . . . . . . . . . . . . . . . . . . . . . . . . . .68
**52** Felting Tools . . . . . . . . . . . . . . . . . . . . . . . . . . . .69

**Chapter 5**

## SERGER SENSATIONS

**53** Serger Tweezers ........................72

**54** Looper Threader ........................73

**55** Thread Nets...........................74

**56** Seam Sealants ........................75

**57** Bob 'n Serge ..........................76

**58** Serger Seam Rippers...................77

**59** Scrap Catcher.........................78

**60** Serger Foot Pads ......................79

**61** Canned Air—Serger Upkeep Necessities .....80

**62** Mini Vacuum Attachments—
Serger Upkeep Necessities..................81

**63** Serger Brushes—Serger Upkeep Necessities..81


**Chapter 6**

## SEW, PRESS, SEW, PRESS

**64** Irons................................84

**65** Pressing Surfaces .....................86

**66** Ironing Spray ........................87

**67** Fabric Press Cloth .....................88

**68** Appliqué Pressing Sheet.................88

**69** Pressing Boards ......................89

**70** Padded Pressing Notions ...............90

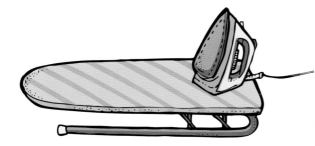

**Chapter 7**

## ONE-TASK WONDERS

**71** Bias-Tape Makers..........................94

**72** Pocket Templates .....................95

**73** Bodkins..............................96

**74** SimFlex Expanding Gauge ................97

**75** Pattern Notchers......................98

**76** Chenille Cutters.......................99

**77** Portable Bobbin Winders .................99

**78** Light Boxes .........................100

**79** No-Math Miter........................101

**80** Telescoping Extension Magnets .........102

**81** Hot-Fix Applicator Wands................103

**82** Tube Turners........................104

**83** Flexible Curve Rulers...................106

**84** French Curve Rulers....................107

**85** Fashion Design Kits ...................107

**86** Hem Markers .......................108

**87** Hem Gauges........................109

**88** Needle Sharpeners ...................110

**89** Pressing Bars........................111

**Chapter 8**

## FAVORITE FEET

**90** Open-Toe Foot.......................114

**91** ¼" Quilting Foot .....................115

**92** Free-Motion Quilting Foot ..............116

**93** Walking Foot........................117

**94** Edge-Joining Foot ....................118

**95** Piping Foot .........................118

**96** Overcast-Guide Foot...................119

**97** Pin-Tuck Foot .......................119

**98** Fringe Foot .........................120

**99** Multicord Foot.......................120

**100** Ruffler Foot.........................121

## THE MOST IMPORTANT NOTION

**101** A Sewing Buddy .........................122


**Notion Index**

Listing of all notions included in book ..........124

# 1

# Gotta-Have Notions

Gotta-have notions are those notions of necessity that make your sewing easier and more enjoyable for a multitude of projects. I have included my all-time favorites, new innovations and what the professionals use to improve their sewing results in the most efficient way.

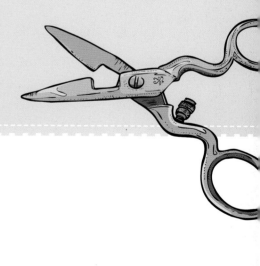

# MARKING PENS

Every sewing or quilting hobbyist needs an assortment of marking tools. Accurate marking is one of the secrets to professional-looking projects. Marking actually saves you time because project pieces align with ease.

A fine-point pen makes it much easier to mark fine lines, trace small designs and transfer complex pattern marks. Water-erasable, air-erasable or white marking pens—decisions, decisions, decisions... Here is a guide to help you decide when to use each.

## Air-Erasable Pen

**Features:**

The air-erasable pen makes bright purple or pink marks that usually vanish in twelve to twenty-four hours without washing. Pressing can permanently set marks, so remove marks with water before pressing.

**Use:**

Use an air-erasable pen when marking washable fabric or embroidery that you plan to sew right away. If you mark your project and decide to sew it at a later time, your marks most likely will be gone.

## Water-Erasable Pen

**Features:**

This pin-point pen makes fine lines, so you can trace small designs or mark complex patterns clearly. A water-erasable pen makes bright blue marks that are easily removed with plain water. Pressing can permanently set marks, so remove marks with water before pressing.

**Use:**

Mark embroidery, quilting and pattern details on washable fabrics.

*Fine-Point Water-Erasable Pen*

*Air-Erasable Pen*

*Water-Erasable Marking Pen*

*White Marking Pen*

## White Marking Pen

**Features:**

This fine-point pen clearly marks dark fabrics. As the ink dries, white markings become more visible. Markings disappear upon ironing or when you spritz with water.

**Use:**

This is my very favorite! For years, I wondered why there wasn't a white marking pen available; when this came out, I was thrilled! I use it on dark fabric—quilt blocks, pattern details and craft projects. I especially like the fact that marks disappear when I iron the project.

## NOTE from NANCY

Regardless of what type of marker you use, always test marking and removing the mark on a scrap of fabric before marking your project. Remove marks with ease using a dual marking pen. These pens are available as air- or water-erasable. A pen is at one end of the marker and an eraser at the other, so you can make your mark and immediately erase it.

Chalk is perfect to use on fabrics with a nap or when marking with a ruler. A marker with a rotating metal chalk wheel snugs up close to the ruler and produces a clean, accurate mark.

## Tailor's Chalk

**Features:**
Tailor's chalk is often found in the shape of a triangle; the edge marks fabric with precision. The marks are easily removed and don't leave a residue. The chalk is usually available in several colors. Tailor's chalk may have a chalky or waxy consistency. Some Tailor's chalk comes with a sharpener to maintain pointed edges for fine line marking.

**Uses:**
Tailor's chalk is a classic! It works on just about any fabric. However, because it is easily removed, it may not be the best choice on fabrics that are handled a lot.

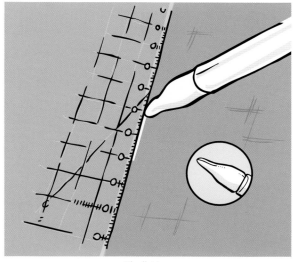

*Chalk Liner*

## Chalk Liner

**Features:**
The tapered end on this marking tool dispenses a thin line of chalk from a rotating wheel. Markings easily brush or wash away. They come in different colors: blue, pink, white and yellow. There are several variations of this tool on the market; the only difference is the shape of the case.

**Use:**
These chalk liners are great for drawing both straight lines and freehand curves. Use on washable fabrics only, as dry-cleaning may make the marks permanent.

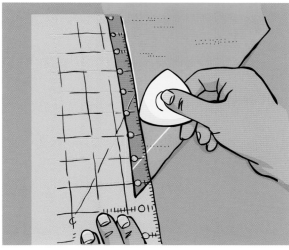

*Tailor's Chalk*

### BUDGET FRIENDLY option

Bar soap isn't chalk, but it can be used to mark many of the same fabrics as chalk, plus it is readily available. Be frugal and save small soap slivers to mark dark washable fabrics! Use a knife to carefully trim soap ends for a sharp edge. Avoid soap that contains oil to avoid staining your fabric. Ivory soap is an ideal brand because it doesn't have a lot of additives.

I still love to use a good, old-fashioned tracing wheel and marking paper for marking darts, pleats and placement lines on the wrong side of my fabric. It is fast and accurate!

*Blunt Serrated -Edge Tracing Wheel*

## Blunt Serrated-Edge Tracing Wheel

**Features:**

A blunt serrated-edge tracing wheel marks lines clearly and helps preserve pattern tissue and tracing paper.

**Uses:**

The blunt serrated-edge gives you more control of the tracing wheel. The serrated edge grips the fabric, leaving marks that are more accurate.

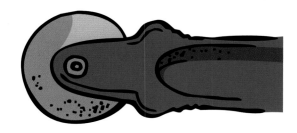

*Blunt Smooth-Edge Tracing Wheel*

## Blunt Smooth-Edge Tracing Wheel

**Features:**

A blunt smooth-edge tracing wheel looks much like a mini pizza cutter. It doesn't seem to mark as accurately for curved pattern pieces but works well when used with a straight-edge for straight lines.

**Uses:**

Use for marks made in conjunction with a ruler for quilting and craft projects.

*Needlepoint Tracing Wheel*

## Needlepoint Tracing Wheel

**Features:**

A needlepoint tracing wheel has a pinpoint edge to quickly pierce through paper patterns. You are able to mark fabric with an erasable pen or pencil following the pinpoint perforations.

**Uses:**

The primary use of a needlepoint tracing wheel is for drafting patterns and copying designs. Quickly trace patterns onto pattern paper with this handy notion.

# Tracing Paper

**Features:**

The surface of tracing paper may be waxed or water-soluble. Tracing-paper packs usually contain several colored sheets that can be used multiple times. Position the tracing paper with the waxy side toward the fabric to be marked. Transfer the paper colors to fabric by rolling a tracing wheel over the paper. Water-soluble tracing-paper markings remove easily with a damp cloth, while those from waxed tracing paper may be a little more difficult to remove.

**Uses:**

Tracing paper allows you to transfer sewing, quilting or embroidery pattern markings with ease. My favorite is Clover Chacopy Tracing Paper because it has a nice assortment of colors and the marks are distinctive, yet easy to remove.

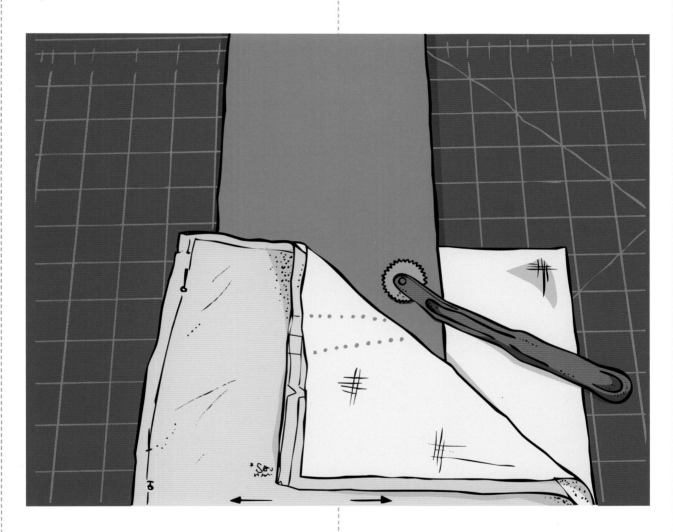

Stitch with perfection when you use a seam guide! Your stitching lines and seams will be straight and accurate with the help of this gotta-have notion. These guides are especially useful for someone learning to sew, as sewing involves eye-hand coordination skills that develop with practice.

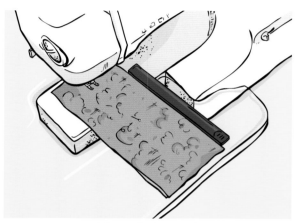

*Adhesive Quilting Guide*

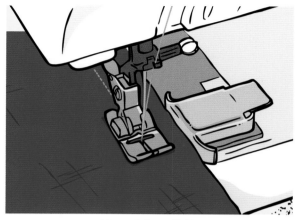

*Magnetic Seam Guide*

## Adhesive Quilting Guide

**Features:**

Adhere this guide to the bed of your sewing machine. It provides a ³⁄₁₆" thick wall that helps you to sew accurate and straight lines. This acrylic guide measures ⅝" × 6" and is reusable. Any sewing machine can use this guide, and it will not harm computerized sewing machines. Replacement adhesive strips are available, but adhesive will last much longer if you place the guide in a plastic bag when not in use to keep the adhesive from drying out.

**Uses:**

Use this guide to stitch a perfectly straight line every time. It is especially helpful for the fold-and-finish reversible quilting technique used by Betty Cotton.

## Magnetic Seam Guide

**Features:**

A magnetic seam guide attaches to the metal throat plate on your sewing machine to ensure a uniform seam width. The guide adjusts to a variety of seam widths and removes easily. If your machine has computerized parts, please check your instruction manual to see if a magnetic guide may be used on your machine.

**Uses:**

Use this guide to stitch a perfectly straight line, as with the adhesive guide. No adhesive to replace!

### NOTE from NANCY

I'm stuck on sticky notes! Take the brown backing sheet off the notepad and stick the whole pad to your machine with the binding side facing the needle. Guide your fabric along the edge of the pad. It's reusable! Simply tear off the bottom sheet if the pad needs to be more tacky. Plus, you can take notes as you stitch!

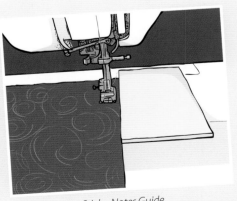

*Sticky-Notes Guide*

This "weigh in" is a positive one! Pattern weights are definitely more convenient and easier to use than pins, especially when dressmaking. I prefer to use weights in conjunction with pins to secure my tissue pattern pieces to fabric for cutting. I use pins to secure pattern grainline and foldline areas, and I use several weights to secure the remaining pattern.

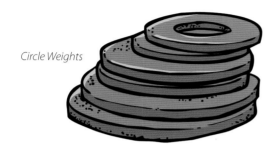

*Circle Weights*

## NOTE from NANCY

Four weights (the usual amount in a package) really are not enough when working on a project, especially if you have a large cutting area. I prefer to have eight to twelve.

## Circle Weights

**Features:**

Circle weights measure about 2¾" in diameter and have a hole in the center. They are brightly colored to make them stand out on your pattern or fabric. Each of the weights has small plastic points on the bottom to eliminate shifting during use. They stack nicely, and an organizer is available to store them.

**Uses:**

Weights are great not only for pattern tissues, but also for anchoring large pieces of fabric to keep them from slipping off your cutting table. The plastic points on the bottom of these weights are very helpful in holding fabric in place. Weights also work well for holding the layers of a quilt or wall hanging together while pinning.

## Canvas Weights

**Features and Uses:**

These colorful pattern weights are the newest "heavy-weight" in the notions scene. They are easy to grasp and ideal for delicate fabrics that often snag on pins. They are usually made of heavy canvas and filled with buckshot.

*Canvas Weights*

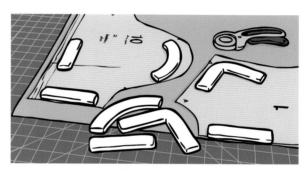

*Shaped Weights*

## Shaped Weights

**Features:**

These pattern weights are designed to fit common curves and shapes of pattern pieces. Curved, right-angle and straight weights are usually included in a set. They have a somewhat rounded top and flat bottom and are quite heavy.

**Uses:**

Use straight weights for long pattern areas, curved weights for armhole or other curves and right-angle weights for hems and angular pattern areas. I like to use them for dressmaking because they are larger than most weights, and I prefer the shaped weights on pattern tissue.

### BUDGET FRIENDLY option

Try using heavy washers or cans of tuna to replace purchased pattern weights. A great perk is that you can invite a friend for tuna salad after all your cutting is completed!

# PINCUSHIONS

Store your pins on a pincushion that is practical or novel—whatever suits your fancy and is efficient to use. Pick a pincushion that sharpens your pins and needles, organizes them, keeps them from rusting or just looks cute!

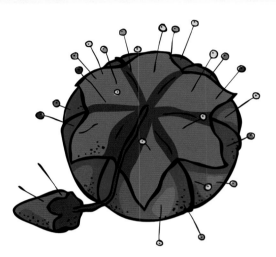

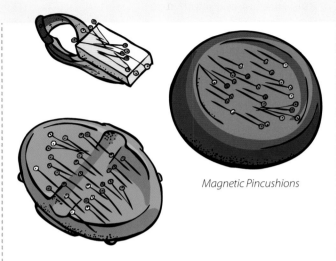

*Magnetic Pincushions*

## Fabric Pincushions

**Features:**

Find a fabric pincushion that is soft or colorful or that coordinates with your sewing area. There are many on the market, including the old standby tomato pincushion with attached strawberry. The strawberry is usually filled with silica sand or emery powder that sharpens your needles. Small stuffed purses, cupcakes, shoes, flowers and fruit are among the new novelties, while a felted wool cushion serves to lubricate and protect pins from rust and corrosion because of the lanolin in the wool.

**Uses:**

Organize, store, clean and sharpen your pins with a fabric pincushion. Fabric pincushions are especially useful for stainless steel pins that will not adhere to a magnetic pincushion.

## Magnetic Pincushions

**Features:**

Magnetic pincushions are colorful and easy to use. They can also be used to hold paper clips, safety pins or other small metal items, except for stainless steel. They are great for the office as well as the sewing room!

**Uses:**

Magnetic pin keepers and dispensers keep pins together without having to place them on a fabric cushion one by one.

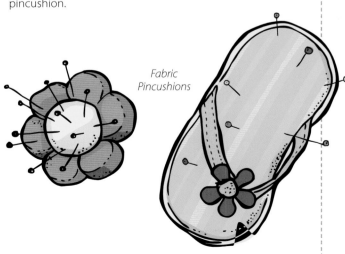

*Fabric Pincushions*

Don't be afraid to make a mistake—learn the mantra "As ye sew, so shall ye rip!" Remove unwanted stitches from your project with an unsung hero, the seam ripper. All sewers and quilters learn "reverse sewing" at some point in their creative endeavors. Seam ripper designs are numerous. Some fold out like a pocketknife, while others have a cover that slips over the blade. In the list of the most innovative seam rippers is one that has a magnifier attached, and another that features a light to assist with vision on dark fabrics. Choose the best-quality and sharpest seam ripper for your sewing room. It is definitely a must-have notion!

## Ergonomic Seam Ripper

**Features:**

Many ergonomic seam rippers measure about 5½" long. The rounded design fits comfortably in your hand, and the blade is electronically ground for permanent sharpness and features a safety ball at one end to protect fabric.

**Uses:**

The design of the ergonomic seam ripper makes it easy to handle when removing seams and stitches, cutting buttonholes, removing snaps and opening buttonholes.

## Seam Ripper Clipper

**Features:**

An advantage of a seam ripper clipper is that its angled nose can get into a seam and remove stitches without ripping the fabric. This spring action tool makes clipping easy and also eliminates hand fatigue. You'll wonder how you ever got along without this handy rip it and clip it tool!

**Uses:**

Use the seam ripper clipper to rip seams and clip thread tails with one tool.

## 12-in-1 Multi Tool

**Features and Uses:**

This handy tool includes not only a seam ripper but also a magnifying glass, measuring tape, stuffing tool, thread cutter, tweezers, punch needle, safety pin, piercing punch, knit picker and two needle threaders—all in one compact package. Have all the tools you need, right at your fingertips!

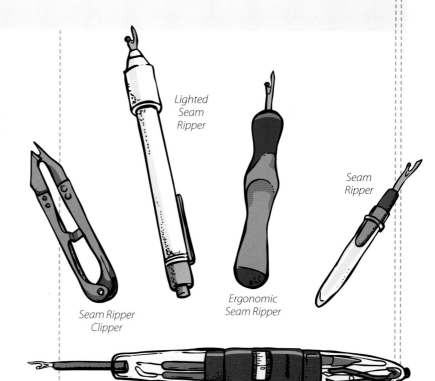

*Lighted Seam Ripper*

*Seam Ripper*

*Seam Ripper Clipper*

*Ergonomic Seam Ripper*

*12-in-1 Multi Tool*

## NOTE from NANCY

Use a seam ripper for multiple functions in or out of the sewing room. Remember that using it for jobs it wasn't intended for may quickly dull the seam ripper, so it is best to have several inexpensive varieties on hand. Keep a seam ripper in the kitchen for removing labels from cans, one with your pet supplies to cut burrs from your dog's fur, and possibly another with your mailing supplies to help open packages.

In my lifetime I have used more of these little pieces of metal wire than any other sewing notion. You can never have too many pins! Fitting, layering, marking, basting and more—pins do it all. The variety of pins is mind-boggling. Only my personal favorites are mentioned here. The main considerations in choosing pins for a project are length, thickness, and type of head and tip, plus metal preference. The most important feature is that they are sharp with no burrs. Lengths range from 8–34mm (approximately ½"–3¾").

## Dressmaker Pins

**Features:**

Dressmaker pins are designed to be used with light- to medium-weight fabrics. They are typically size 20 (1¼") with metal heads.

**Uses:**

Use dressmaker pins for securing pattern layers and seams, pinning garments for alterations, pin-marking sewing projects, pin-basting a garment and much more. Use a traditional pincushion with stainless steel pins because they are not attracted to a magnet. See Pincushions on page 14.

## Flat-Head Pins

**Features:**

These 2" long pins have a flat plastic head and a sharp tip to glide through fabric smoothly.

**Uses:**

Flat-head pins are especially useful for hand work, pinning lace and other loose weaves and pinning lofty fabrics such as fleece. I especially like to use flat-head pins on projects that will be cut with a rotary cutter so the straightedge stays level in the cutting process. The flat head is convenient for ironing, but it is best to avoid heat directly on the plastic head to prevent melting.

## Quilting Pins

**Features:**

Glasshead quilting pins are the ultimate! They measure 1⅞", which is perfect for pinning many quilt layers. The glass head will not melt from the heat of an iron, and the super-fine steel shank has a precision sharp point.

**Uses:**

These pins are made especially for pinning a multitude of fabric and batting layers but are also good for garment making. The long length keeps them from slipping out of place, and the superfine points let you pin a variety of fabrics without snagging.

## Appliqué Pins

**Features:**

Appliqué pins are approximately ½"–¾" long and may have a metal or glass head.

**Uses:**

This shorter pin is perfect for appliqué projects, trims and sequins or beads. You are less likely to poke yourself while maneuvering small appliqué pieces as you stitch when you use these short pins. The glass heads allow you to iron without the fear of melting a pinhead.

## NOTE from NANCY

Many pins are labeled "rustproof" or "rust resistant." However, if you store pinned fabric in an area that has a high moisture level, it is very likely that the pins may still rust and damage your fabric. This is especially true in areas near the ocean where the environment is moist and salty.

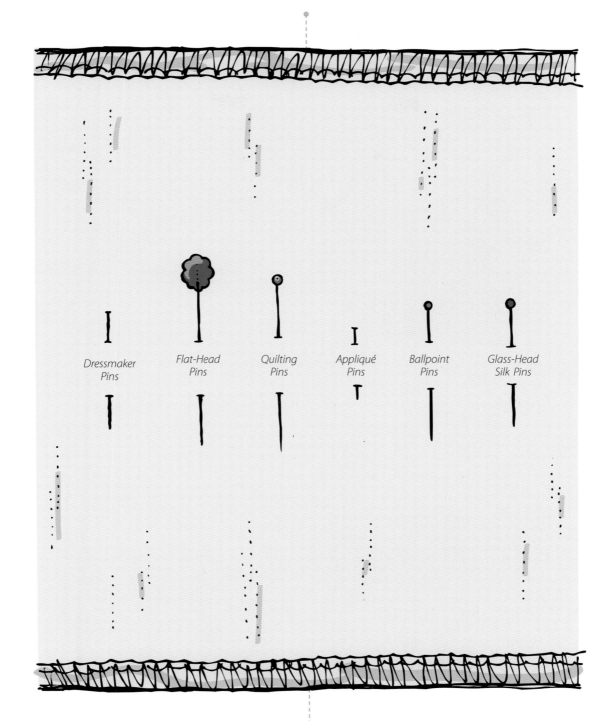

Dressmaker Pins

Flat-Head Pins

Quilting Pins

Appliqué Pins

Ballpoint Pins

Glass-Head Silk Pins

## Ballpoint Pins

**Features:**

Extra-fine ballpoint pins have a rounded tip so they are able to slip between the loops of knit fabric without piercing or pulling the yarns. Ballpoint pins have large multicolor plastic or metal heads, and sizes range from 1¹⁄₁₆"–1¾". Pins are available in nickel-plated steel or stainless steel.

**Uses:**

Use with knits and lingerie fabrics.

## Glass-Head Silk Pins

**Features:**

These colored glass-head pins measure approximately 1⅜" and have a superfine steel shank. The heads will not melt under the heat of an iron.

**Uses:**

Use on delicate fabrics for projects requiring a longer pin.

# BUTTONHOLE CUTTERS

Neatly cut buttonholes give your garment a handmade rather than "homemade" appearance. You can use small sharp scissors, buttonhole scissors, a seam ripper or a buttonhole chisel and mat. The right tool is the one that works best for you—a tool that is fast and efficient.

*Chisel and Mat*

*Buttonhole Scissors*

## Chisel and Mat

**Features:**

Chisel blades are sharp, and sturdy handles with gripper inserts allow excellent control for cutting buttonholes. A set usually includes a straight cutter, keyhole cutter and small square mat or wood block. Protective covers are a must for these sharp blades! The blade on a straight cutter is approximately ½" wide.

**Uses:**

Cut straight buttonholes with the straight blade, eyelets with the keyhole blade and keyhole buttonholes with a combination of the straight and keyhole blades. The keyhole blade also works well for decorative cutting on fabrics such as synthetic suede.

## Buttonhole Scissors

**Features:**

Use buttonhole scissors just like your grandmother used to use! A new pair of 4½" buttonhole scissors is a revival from the past and cuts a perfect buttonhole every time without damaging the buttonhole threads. Determine the exact length for the buttonhole cut on scrap fabric and adjust the screw to calibrate that length. Each and every buttonhole cut with that calibration is the same length.

**Uses:**

Use buttonhole scissors to cut uniform buttonholes on light- or medium-weight fabrics.

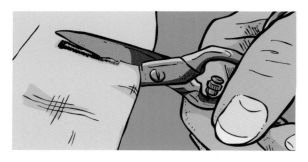

### BUDGET FRIENDLY option

Place your fabric on a hard surface and use the back side of a seam ripper's tip to score the buttonhole. Insert the seam ripper to cut the buttonhole; there will be a slight resistance at the end of your scoring line, which helps prevent cutting through the end of the buttonhole.

Whether you collect thimbles or actually use them, the value far exceeds the cost! Decorative or purposeful, there's a thimble to suit everyone!

*Standard Thimbles*

*Ring Thimble*

## Standard Thimbles

**Features:**
Thimbles are used to push a needle through layers of fabric while protecting your finger. They may be used on whichever finger suits your fancy. You'll find thimbles made of metal, porcelain, wood and glass, among other materials. Metal thimbles use a sizing system that ranges from 6–12. Sizes 6–8 are size small, 9–11 are medium and 12 is large. Size on a metal thimble is frequently imprinted on the inside of the thimble top. Porcelain and other thimbles are not usually sized. The indentations on the tips and sides of the thimble help you secure the needle to push it through the fabric. A ring thimble is a variation that leaves the tip of your finger free to grasp the needle.

**Uses:**
Use a thimble when hand sewing or quilting to protect your finger from being pricked as you sew and to help coax the needle through layered or thick fabric.

## Leather Thimbles

**Features:**
Leather thimbles feature a metal tip for guiding the needle through various thicknesses of fabric. The soft leather molds to the shape of your finger and helps you control your needle as you sew. There is often an open tip that allows your fingernail to extend without changing the thimble length.

**Uses:**
A leather thimble is perfect for sewing or quilting by hand. You'll wonder how you ever got along without it!

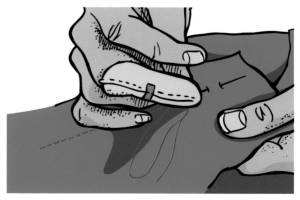

*Leather Thimble*

# SEAM GAUGES

A seam gauge is perfect for measuring those areas that need a small, firm ruler rather than a tape measure. Some have the added feature of a sliding marker to keep a hem or seam even while pinning or sewing.

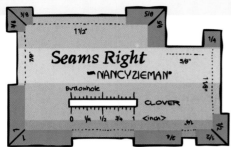

*Mini Measurement Gauge*

*1" × 6" Ruler*

*6" Seam Gauge*

## 6" Seam Gauge

**Features:**

A 6" seam gauge is usually made of metal and has a metal or plastic sliding marker to keep an even measurement when pinning or sewing.

**Uses:**

Try this gotta-have notion for measuring seams, hems and other small measurements with ease and accuracy. Decide on a measurement, set the sliding marker and measure.

## Mini Measurement Gauge

**Features:**

Each edge of this convenient gauge sports another commonly used measurement. This miniature gauge saves time when measuring small standard sewing increments.

**Uses:**

This handy tool is easier to use than a regular ruler to quickly mark seam allowances, ranging from ¼" to 1⅛", and to mark buttonholes with the easy view slot.

## 1" x 6" Ruler

**Features:**

This frosted plastic ruler has black lines in ⅛" increments for precision marking.

**Uses:**

The 1" × 6" nonslip ruler works well on both light and dark fabric because of the frosted surface. Use it for small quilting projects or for garment sewing when you need precise measurements.

## 5-in-1 Tool

**Features:**

This gauge is really five separate notions, including a T-gauge, hem gauge, circle compass, buttonhole spacer and seam allowance gauge.

**Uses:**

Use the 5-in-1 tool for the following sewing and quilting tasks:

- Space and place buttonholes and buttons accurately.
- Measure and mark seam allowances with adjustable ⅛" notched increments.
- Get straight and even hem measurements.
- Create perfect circles with the circle compass.
- Measure precise right angles with the T-gauge.

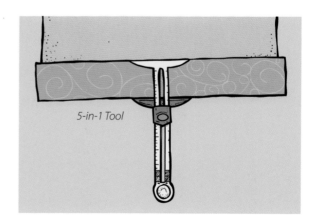

*5-in-1 Tool*

### NOTE from NANCY

In the past I've used five different tools to do the job of this one gauge. Whether quilting or sewing, I find it a versatile and accurate tool to measure, mark and create. Now that's a streamlined gotta-have notion!

An inexpensive flexible tape measure is easy to find and easy to use! It is often printed with advertising information and given away at various promotional events.

*Standard Tape Measure*

*Retractable Tape Measure*

## Standard Tape Measure

**Features:**
Choose a 60" or 120" long tape measure made of durable plastic, cloth or nonstretch fiberglass. Metal or plastic tips on the ends of the tape measure protect it from fraying. Most tape measures are marked with inches on one side and centimeters on the other.

**Uses:**
Measure your body for pattern alterations or measure your pattern grainline. A flexible ruler is indispensable for sewing—a dressmaker's friend! You can even stand it on its side and measure curves, corners or the circumference of a circle.

## Retractable Tape Measure

**Features:**
Most spring tape measures are 60" long, are made of fiberglass and come nestled in a plastic case. Some are marked in both metric and American measurements.

**Uses:**
A retractable tape measure is a convenient version of the standard tape measure. The tape recoils easily into its plastic or metal case for easy storage in a pocket or purse.

**NOTE from NANCY**

Standard tape measures are ⅝" wide. That's good to know when you need a quick seam gauge!

**NOTE from NANCY**

Grandmothers have told me that the magical appearing and hiding of that spring tape has quieted many grandchildren—always keep one in your purse!

Threading needles can try your patience and waste precious time. A thin, flexible looped wire forms one of the most time-saving notions—the needle threader! Place the loop of the needle threader through the eye of the needle, insert an inch or two of thread through the loop and gently pull the needle threader back out of the needle along with the thread. Voilà! Your needle is ready for a "stitch in time"!

## Diamond-Shaped Needle Threader

**Features:**

This looped wire needle threader has been bent into a diamond shape and attached to a plastic or metal handle.

**Uses:**

Place the needle threading wire through the eye of a needle; it opens into a large diamond, making it easy to pass the thread through. Pull the wire back through the eye of the needle, bringing the thread along with it.

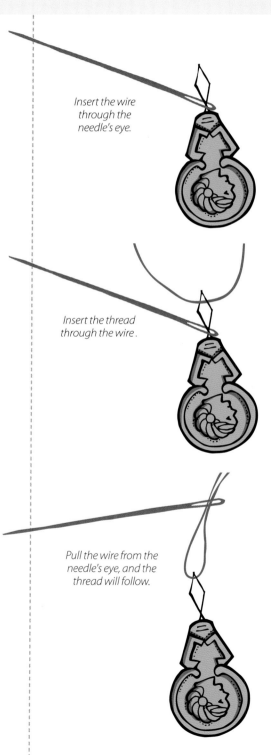

*Insert the wire through the needle's eye.*

*Insert the thread through the wire.*

*Pull the wire from the needle's eye, and the thread will follow.*

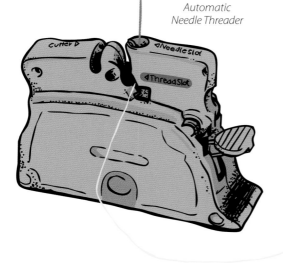

*Automatic Needle Threader*

## Spiral Eye Needle

**Features:**

This one-of-a-kind American-made Spiral Eye Needle is relatively new and has won several awards. The opening is at the side, so it stays threaded when you are pulling your stitches. It is made of solid metal, so you can sharpen it instead of throwing it out when it becomes dull.

**Uses:**

Loop the thread over the Spiral Eye Needle and slide it toward the slot. Tug the thread into the slot and toward the eye of the needle, and you are ready to sew! These needles are especially useful for people with limited vision or arthritis and for children learning to sew. Plus, they eliminate the need for a needle threader.

*Spiral Eye Needle*

## Automatic Needle Threader

**Features:**

This colorful, plastic desktop needle threader usually measures 1" wide × 3" long × 2¼" high.

**Uses:**

You can thread most handsewing needles using the automatic needle threader at just the push of a button!

## NOTE from NANCY

I recommend using a Spiral Eye Needle to bury threads on a quilt top after machine quilting is complete. They are wonderful to secure a short thread and hide it in the fabric layers.

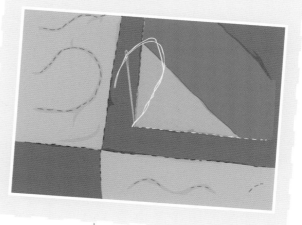

Position and insert your sewing machine needle with ease! A needle inserter is a plastic wand with a tapered hole to hold a needle in place as you position it in your sewing machine or serger. If you have ever dropped a needle you were trying to insert into your sewing machine or serger, you might call this a magic wand! The needle inserter is a handy tool because the narrow wand fits where your fingers won't. Some inserters have a brush on the other end, but my favorite has a wire needle threader on the opposite end.

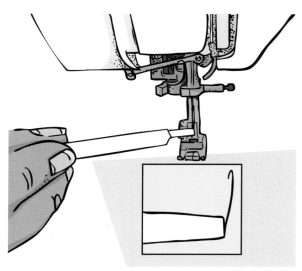

*Needle Inserter and Threader*

## Needle Inserter and Threader

**Features:**
A needle inserter is designed to hold a needle as you insert or remove it from your machine. You are less likely to drop the needle down into the machine when you use this handy tool. The opposite end of the needle inserter wand may feature a brush or needle threader.

**Uses:**
Use the tapered hole on one end of the narrow plastic wand to insert a needle, and the brush on the opposite end to gently brush the lint from your needle and bobbin case area. Some needle inserters have a needle threader hook on the opposite end. Place the wire hook through your needle from back to front. Place thread over the hook and draw it into the eye of the needle by pulling the wire threader back through the eye of the needle.

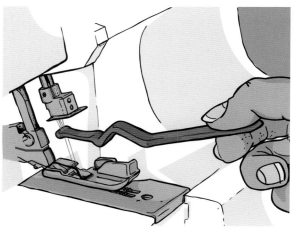

*Two-Needle Installer*

## Two-Needle Installer

**Features:**
This handy plastic wand has two tapered holes for inserting or removing needles, and was designed to be used with a serger. Most two-needle installers are brightly colored to make them easy to find!

**Uses:**
Use one hole when inserting or removing a single needle, and two holes for inserting or removing two needles. Rest your index finger under the bend in the plastic wand to give you more leverage when positioning needles.

### NOTE from NANCY

There are several types of needle inserters and threaders—many sewing machines and sergers come with them, so check your accessory box. Keep a needle inserter and threader handy, as it is a great time saver.

The power of a hemostat or pliers is brought to your sewing room courtesy of these great notions—and they're designed with the sewer/quilter/crafter in mind. Gotta have 'em!

*Needle Gripper*

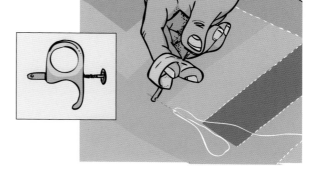

*Needle Puller*

## Needle Gripper

**Features:**

A needle gripper's serrated tips hold needles and thread securely, and many handles are designed to be comfortable for larger fingers or arthritic hands. Some grippers also have a sturdy self-locking clamp.

**Uses:**

A needle gripper helps grip and remove thread, change needles, clamp fabric, remove tangled bobbin thread and tighten set screws.

## Needle Puller

**Features:**

This 2" x 2" needle puller features molded plastic finger grips and a metal plunger and tip.

**Uses:**

This unique tool works like pliers to pull a needle through heavy or layered fabric—but with more finesse. Place a needle into the small hole at the tip of the puller, press on the spring-loaded plunger to secure the needle and pull the needle from the fabric. It works like magic!

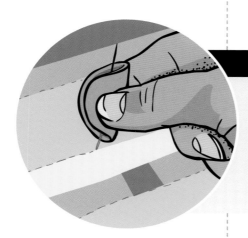

### BUDGET FRIENDLY option

Purchase an inexpensive rubber gripper made for opening jars. Use scissors to trim sections of the gripper to make small needle-gripping mats. These small grippers are especially useful when tying quilts, to pull a needle threaded with yarn or ribbon through multiple layers.

# SHEARS/SCISSORS

Buy the best-quality shears and scissors you can afford. Your sewing projects will thank you!

Shears are best for cutting out your patterns because the blades are longer (over 6" in length). Shears have one large hole for two or three fingers and a smaller hole for your thumb, whereas scissors have two smaller holes. The grip on shears allows you to cut for longer periods of time without hand fatigue. Shears are designed specifically for right- or left-hand use.

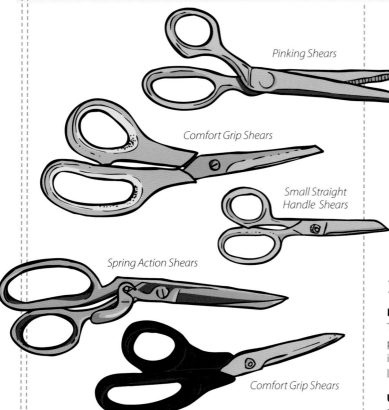

*Pinking Shears*

*Comfort Grip Shears*

*Small Straight Handle Shears*

*Spring Action Shears*

*Comfort Grip Shears*

## NOTE from NANCY

I prefer bent-handle, knife-edge shears. The bent handle allows you to cut smoothly across a flat surface. The advantage of knife-edge shears is that they easily glide through the fabric. With knife-edge shears, you can cock them half-open and zip through a length of fabric. A disadvantage: The blades need sharpening a bit more often than standard shears.

## Dressmaker's Shears

**Features:**
The longer blades of shears are strong enough to cut through multiple layers of fabric. The handles are either bent or straight and may be metal or molded nylon for a more comfortable grip. The metals used for shears vary; however, double-plated chrome over nickel or high-carbon stainless steel are popular choices. The new spring-action shears reduce fatigue when cutting because the blades gently open after each cut.

**Uses:**
Dressmaker's shears are ideal for cutting out patterns and trimming seams, though they are used primarily to cut multiple layers of fabric.

## Pinking Shears

**Features:**
These shears feature a characteristic zigzag-edge blade to produce a ravel-resistant edge on seams or decorative edging on craft projects. Pinking shears are designed to cut one layer of fabric at a time, for all practical purposes.

**Uses:**
Pinking shears are used mainly for creating a decorative finish on no-fray fabrics or to produce a ravel-resistant edge on garment or craft seams.

## Microserrated-Edge Shears

**Features:**
These shears have all the features of the dressmaker's shears; plus, the knife edge is serrated to grip slippery fabrics while cutting. The points of the shears are slightly blunted to avoid snagging fabric.

**Uses:**
Microserrated-edge shears are especially useful for knits and other fabrics that tend to slip when cutting.

*Microserrated-Edge*

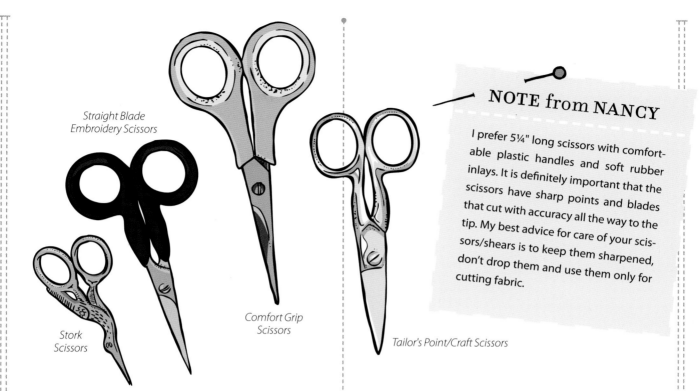

*Straight Blade Embroidery Scissors*

*Stork Scissors*

*Comfort Grip Scissors*

*Tailor's Point/Craft Scissors*

## Scissors

**Features:**

The shorter blades of good-quality scissors should cut all the way to the tip. The handles are usually straight and may be metal, molded nylon or plastic. They may feature soft rubber inlays for comfort. The metals used for scissors vary; however, double-plated chrome over nickel or durable stainless steel are popular choices.

**Uses:**

Scissors with sharp points are perfect for cutting detailed appliqués, fussy-cutting, ripping seams and snipping threads. Most scissors are designed to be used in either hand.

## Appliqué Scissors

**Features:**

The "pelican bill" on these scissors fans the lower layer of fabric away from the upper layer for an accurate close cut.

**Uses:**

Use appliqué scissors to trim multiple layers of fabric. They are ideal for use in appliqué work and grading seams.

## Spring Action Scissors

**Features:**

These 6½" scissors are made from rust-and-corrosion-resistant high grade steel. Razor-sharp blades make clean and precise cuts. The spring action keeps these scissors in the open position until you secure the blades with the locking clip.

**Uses:**

These heavy-duty scissors easily cut through multiple layers of fabric. A must-have tool for rag quilting and making fleece fringe!

*Spring Action Scissors*

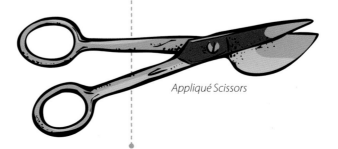

*Appliqué Scissors*

An awl and a stiletto are both used for the same functions—namely, poking holes in needlework or leather work and easing or gripping fabric for stitching. They are made of a variety of materials, including metal, bamboo, bone and porcupine quills. These popular tools become an extension of your hand as you sew.

*Awl*

## Awl or Stiletto

**Features:**

The sharp-pointed tip of an awl is similar to that of a stiletto; however, most stilettos have a long, narrow handle in comparison to an awl's short, thick handle.

**Uses:**

The awl and stiletto are used to guide fabric under the presser foot of your machine, grip straying fabric with the sharp tip, position trims, ease ruffles and gathers and make eyelet holes in needlework, sewing and leather work.

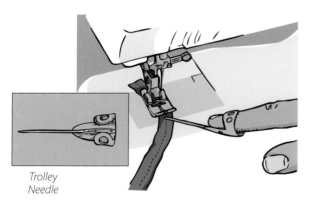

*Trolley Needle*

## Trolley Needle

**Features:**

A trolley needle is a stiletto without the handle. Attach the trolley clip to any fingertip for an ultimate finger extension!

**Uses:**

Smooth your embroidery stitches or guide and grip fabric. And because the trolley needle is attached to your finger, you don't have to drop it and pick it back up as much as with an awl or stiletto. It's the perfect tool to use when sewing ruffles, seams and hems.

### NOTE from NANCY

The most gratifying use for an awl is to punch an extra hole in your belt when you lose weight!

## Sixth Finger Stiletto

**Features:**

Instead of one prong, this modified version of the stiletto has two metal prongs that are split and slanted. One of the prongs is sharp and pointed like a stiletto, and the other is flat.

**Uses:**

Use this handy stiletto to protect your fingers when guiding fabric and trims under the presser foot of your machine, to hold seam allowances open for pressing, to create ribbon-embroidered flowers and stems, to keep fabric from slipping and bunching, and to hold seam allowances flat for joining quilt blocks.

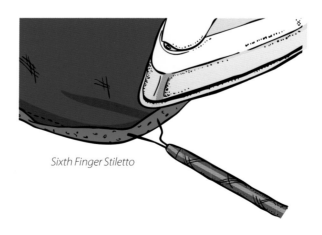

*Sixth Finger Stiletto*

You'll appreciate the ease of using a bodkin for guiding elastic or ribbon through a casing. The blunt tip allows you access in a casing without piercing the fabric or damaging the end of the elastic or ribbon. The length of the tool helps you complete the job quickly and effortlessly, whether you are threading elastic into a casing or a ribbon into delicate eyelet lace.

*Plastic Bodkin*

*Threader and Tweezer Bodkin*

*Safety Pin*

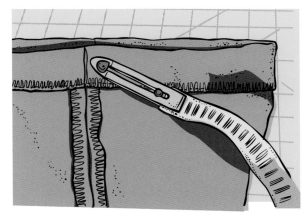

*Wide Bodkin*

## Bodkin

**Features:**

A bodkin looks like a large needle with an oversize eye and a blunt or ballpoint tip. Another version resembles small tongs with grip-like teeth that clench the ribbon or elastic and a sliding ring that slips down the neck of the bodkin to secure the ends.

**Uses:**

Use a bodkin to guide ribbon, elastic or cording through a casing.

## Wide Bodkin

**Features:**

This wide, flat, metal bodkin measures ⅝" × 3". The metal teeth grip onto elastic, cording or fabric strips, and a locking tab secures the bodkin to help slide the strips through a casing without twisting.

**Uses:**

Most regular-sized bodkins are used for narrow ribbon and elastic. A wide bodkin is used for wider elastic, ribbon and fabric strips.

### BUDGET FRIENDLY option

Secure a large safety pin on the end of ribbon or elastic and ease it through a casing. It takes a little more time than a bodkin because it isn't as long and is a little more difficult to grasp, but it works like a charm! Another option is a large tapestry needle.

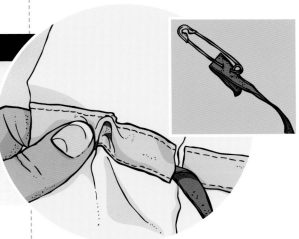

# 2

# Get Organized

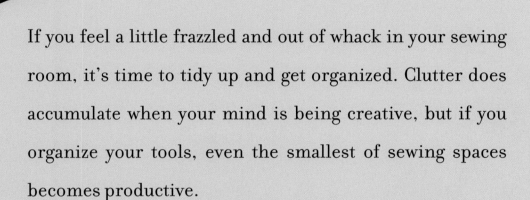

If you feel a little frazzled and out of whack in your sewing room, it's time to tidy up and get organized. Clutter does accumulate when your mind is being creative, but if you organize your tools, even the smallest of sewing spaces becomes productive.

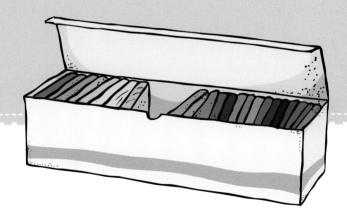

Take the first step in getting organized by lighting up your work area. Natural outside light and ceiling lights are important, but your projects require very specific lighting for color enhancement and eliminating shadows. If you are like me, you can never have enough light, and a magnifier attached to a lamp is like having a stunt double—your eyes don't have to do all the stressful work by themselves!

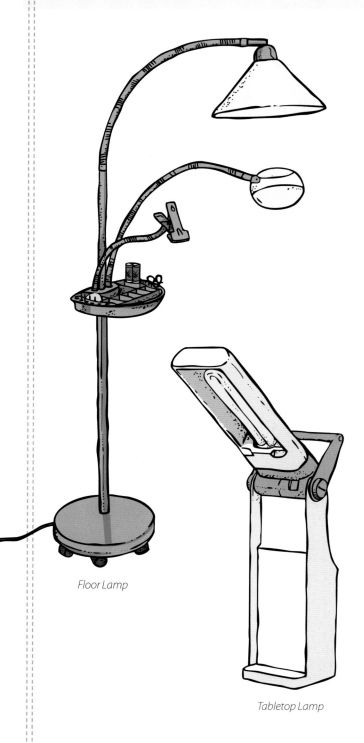

*Floor Lamp*

*Tabletop Lamp*

## Floor Lamp

**Features:**
Nonglare, simulated natural light is best for general task lighting when sewing. Use a flexible neck lamp to position light where needed. Some lamps have flicker-free illumination and attachments such as an accessory tray or a magnifier. Use an 18–60 watt fluorescent or a 130–150 watt incandescent bulb for cutting, marking and machine sewing.

**Uses:**
General overhead lighting illuminates your room, but use task lighting to eliminate shadows and highlight your work areas. Both types of lighting are necessary to reduce eye fatigue and stress.

## Tabletop Lamp

**Features:**
The most desirable type of travel/tabletop lamp emits low-heat, energy-efficient, true-color light. Use a rechargeable battery with an AC adapter when you take your task lamp to class. A low-glare lamp reduces eye strain, and a lamp with adjustable height accommodates the direct light needed for various projects.

**Uses:**
If you love to create, invest in a tabletop lamp. You can take it to class or use it at home for a perfect true-color, direct-lighting source!

This amazing light helps you do your best when sewing challenging or intricate projects.

### Bendable Bright Light

**Features:**

Though there may be similar lamps available, the Bendable Bright Light is my absolute favorite. This task lamp features an LED light assembly with 100,000 light hours and 120 volts. Turn the light on or off with the switch located on the 8' cord. The Bendable Bright Light, with a 5½" flexible arm, attaches to the side of your sewing machine or serger with a nonmagnetic adhesive bracket.

**Uses:**

Light up your sewing area—just where you want it! Shine white light where you need it the most with the flexible neck. Use the Bendable Bright Light for working on dark fabrics, in workshops and in craft areas.

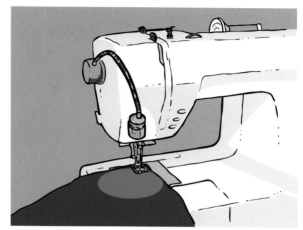

*Bendable Bright Light*

The time-saving serger can create a lot of lint as it stitches and trims. Instead of blowing the lint and fibers deep into your serger parts, use mini vacuum attachments—they're easy to use and work with any vacuum.

*Mini Vacuum Attachments*

### Mini Vacuum Attachments

**Features:**

Mini vacuum attachments typically come in a set, and often include special adapters that attach to any vacuum hose. My favorite set also includes oval and round brushes, a crevice tool and two extensions, which make your cleaning job easier.

**Uses:**

Use these attachments to clean your sewing machine, serger and computer keyboard—the payoff is improved performance!

Organize those small cuts of fabric in convenient bags and boxes that are easily accessible. Sewing is so much more enjoyable when you can grab the fabrics you want and just start sewing rather than having to dig through unorganized boxes, drawers and trunks.

*Fat Quarter Bag*

## Fat Quarter Bag

### Features:

Several types of bags are available, holding anywhere from 60–100 fat quarters that are rolled on cards or folded. The most popular cases are made of waterproof nylon and feature a clear vinyl opening for viewing fabric. Fat quarter bags are easy to clean—just wipe with a damp cloth.

### Uses:

Organize fat quarters by theme, color or collection. Carry fabrics to class using the strong supporting handles.

## Fat Quarter Box

### Features:

One simple fold-together corrugated box designed for fat quarters measures 6" × 8" × 21½" and comes printed with a notions motif. Another fat quarter box measures 7¼" × 11" × 5⅛", holds the fat quarter cards, is collapsible when not in use and includes identification labels.

### Uses:

Any of the boxes designed for fat quarters work well for keeping fat quarters organized and clean.

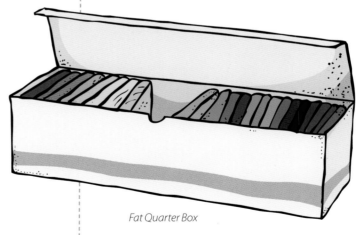

*Fat Quarter Box*

## Fat Quarter Cards and Bands

**Features:**

These white plastic cards feature a center slot for inserting the fabric edge and holes punched at the top of each card to accommodate O-rings.

**Uses:**

Organize fat quarters on the plastic fat quarter cards and secure with nylon fat quarter bands. The bands stretch to accommodate fabric and keep the fabric secure with a hook-and-loop closure. Use cards and bands alone or in a fat quarter bag or box. *Note: Cards and bands are also available for organizing fabric yardage.*

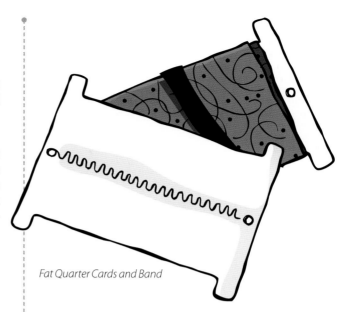

*Fat Quarter Cards and Band*

### BUDGET FRIENDLY option

Use a child's school folder or a manila file folder as a guide for folding fabric. Secure fabric with a large bobby pin and then remove the folder. All these folded fabric bundles are equal in size and easy to stack on shelves or in a cupboard.

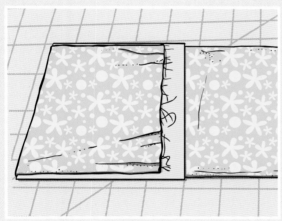

*Fold the fabric in half and then wrap the fabric over a file folder.*

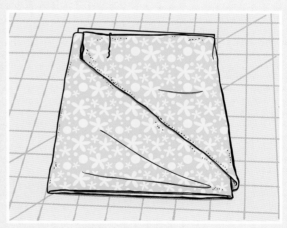

*Tuck the end under diagonally and secure with a bobby pin.*

If you use a rotary cutter, you undoubtedly have an assortment of clear acrylic rulers. Quilters seem to be obsessed with these handy gadgets. Time-saving techniques are of utmost importance, especially when you are working on a large project—a ruler designed for the job is key. Storing rulers for easy access saves precious time; plus, it's a good way to keep your cutting area clean and organized.

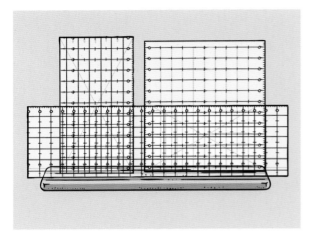

*Tabletop/Hanging Ruler Holder*

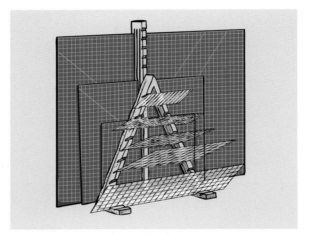

*Ruler and Mat Organizer*

## Tabletop/Hanging Ruler Holder

**Features:**

These organizers have a flat bottom for tabletop use, and a hanger to mount them on the wall. Look for a ruler holder that can hold several different-sized rulers. The slotted wooden ruler holder pictured above has eight slots and measures approximately 7½" × 19".

**Uses:**

Hold rulers upright in slots on a tabletop holder, and slanted in the slots of a hanging holder for easy accessibility. Organize rulers in a holder where they are visible and within easy reach for efficient measuring and cutting as you quilt, sew or craft.

## Ruler, Mat and Tool Organizer

**Features:**

This organizer holds up to 17 rulers and 3 cutting mats in a small compact space. A 15½" tool bar can be added to organize your cutting tools. The organizer measures 8" × 18" × 27".

**Uses:**

Use this ultimate ruler, mat and tool organizer for storage on your tabletop, or hang it with the included hardware.

### BUDGET FRIENDLY option

A simple peg, hook or nail holds most rulers that have a hole in the top. However, when you need the ruler that's on the bottom, you'll need to remove all of the rulers on top of it!

# BOBBIN ORGANIZERS

Have you ever tried to untangle a pile of bobbins? If you have, you know it is very time consuming, unless you wastefully give up and cut the threads. Organize your bobbins in a box, tower or holder designed specifically for them—you'll save time and avoid clutter!

*Bobbin and Spool Organizer*

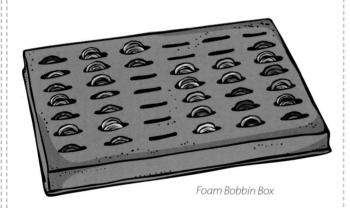

*Foam Bobbin Box*

*Stack 'n Store Bobbin Tower*

## Bobbin and Spool Organizer

**Features:**
Bobbin and spool organizers, such as the Handi-Bob, are usually made of durable plastic. The bobbin holder hooks onto the end of a spool of thread.

**Uses:**
Use these to attach bobbins to matching spools of thread for handy organizing.

## Foam Bobbin Box

**Features:**
Soft, flexible foam bobbin boxes let you easily access your bobbins. The foam holder can be cut to fit your drawers, carrying bags or sewing kits, and it's light enough to take anywhere.

**Uses:**
Use a foam bobbin box, such as a Bobbin Bay, to store your bobbins securely. Bobbins are readily accessible, and the thread color is easily visible. Access your bobbins without untangling a mass of thread!

## Stack 'n Store Bobbin Tower

**Features:**
Neatly store bobbins in this six-layer plastic tower. Stack layers for storage or pull them apart to access a specific bobbin.

**Uses:**
This stackable tower holds and organizes thirty bobbins neatly and efficiently, and holds five bobbins per layer.

### NOTE from NANCY

If you have a narrow drawer in your sewing room, it is the perfect spot to hold several plastic or foam boxes for bobbins. Use a little two-sided tape on the bottom of the boxes, and they won't shift when you open or close the drawer. Marvelous!

Unless you have been fortunate enough to obtain a pattern cabinet from a fabric store or pattern company closeout, pattern boxes are the next best way to organize your patterns.

*Pattern Keepers*

*Pattern Box*

## Pattern Keepers

**Features:**

These 7" × 10" poly bags have a zip closing and are the perfect size for storing a pattern. A special outside pocket holds the pattern envelope or instruction sheet. Inside, pattern pieces are protected, and you have quick access.

**Uses:**

Easily see and access your clothing and craft pattern pieces from the bag and store the pattern envelope in the special outside pocket. Keep each of your patterns neat and organized.

## Pattern Boxes

**Features:**

Choose either a sturdy cardboard or a plastic storage box. Each box typically holds about thirty to forty patterns, and some include dividers. Sizes of the cardboard and plastic boxes vary slightly. Most boxes fold flat when not in use. Some designer styles include intriguing artwork, special handles and reinforced corners.

**Uses:**

Use pattern boxes for organizing and categorizing your pattern collection. Include dividers of your choice for separating the various categories.

### NOTE from NANCY

I like to press each of my pattern pieces so the pattern number shows. It is much easier to find specific pieces without having to unfold each one.

### BUDGET FRIENDLY option

Use file folders with closed sides to store patterns in a regular file cabinet. Some people prefer to adhere the pattern photo to the outside of the file folder. Place the pattern numbers on the file tabs to organize patterns numerically. Use colored folders to further organize patterns by type.

You'll find many different types of thread organizers on the market, but my favorites are still wall-mounted and tabletop thread racks. Some thread organizers take up a lot of precious space in a sewing room.

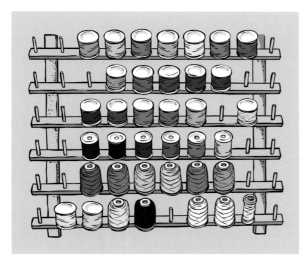

*Wall Thread Rack*

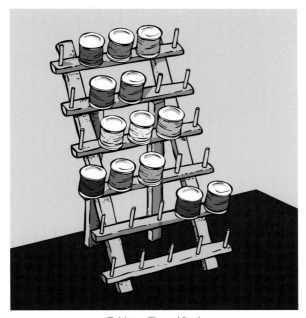

*Tabletop Thread Rack*

## Wall Thread Rack

**Features:**

The racks I am most familiar with hold 60 to 120 spools, but several of them can be linked together for organizing more thread. Use keyhole slots to hang racks on pegboard or heavy-duty picture hangers to hang racks on a wall.

**Uses:**

Sort your thread by color and keep spools neat and tidy with wall thread racks.

## Tabletop Thread Rack

**Features:**

These racks have an easel-type back to allow the rack to stand next to your sewing/embroidery machine. Thirty spool holders are featured on a typical tabletop thread rack, and keyhole slots may be included for a hanging option.

**Uses:**

A tabletop thread rack is handy because you can store your most used thread colors close to your machine. When embroidering, you are able to arrange thread in the order in which you are using it in the design.

### NOTE from NANCY

A little pegboard and several pegged thread organizers work great for organizing your thread. Keep thread clean and dust-free by mounting a sheet of clear vinyl at the top of the organizer to cover thread when not in use.

# TROLLEY ORGANIZERS

Take your sewing machine and projects with you! On-the-go trolley organizers for your sewing machine or serger are perfect to take your machines to class or on a sewing retreat. The padded protection gives you peace of mind, and bringing along your own machine is no longer backbreaking. Some of the newer models allow you to piggyback your serger and your sewing machine so taking two machines is no longer a challenge.

## Sewing-Machine Trolley

**Features:**

Most of these heavy-duty trolleys are fully lined and usually include sturdy nylon straps with padded handles, two heavy-duty rear wheels and two front feet. A retractable handle is a great feature for storage. Inside and outside pockets are definitely a plus for holding projects. Trolley designs accommodate most brands of sewing and embroidery machines. Tapestries and quilted fabrics are very popular choices for trolleys. A waterproof fabric or water-repellent treatment is of utmost importance.

**Uses:**

Use a sewing-machine trolley to wheel your sewing machine to and from your destination with protection for your machine—plus style and comfort for you.

*Serger Trolley*

*Sewing Machine Trolley*

## Serger Trolley

**Features:**

A serger trolley offers convenience and quality along with a stylish appearance. Generous compartments with padded walls can give your serger excellent protection. Look for a fully lined tote with wide nylon straps for comfortable carrying, as well as sturdy feet on the bottom to keep your tote off the ground. Wheels and a retractable handle are a real plus for your trolley. Most serger trolleys fit various brands of machines.

**Uses:**

Use the serger trolley for wheeling your serger to class—it takes that dreaded element of learning how to handle a new machine in the classroom out of the picture.

If you're like me, you need lots of pockets in a tote organizer for all your handy notions. Many notion items are small, but all are essential. Organize your notions by the type of sewing they are used for, and you can just "grab and go" when it's time for class!

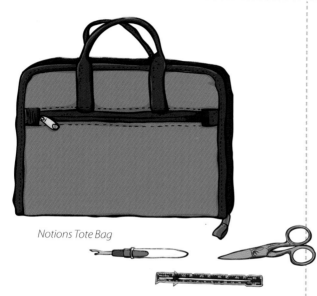

*Notions Tote Bag*

## Embroidery Bag

**Features:**
Store and protect your embroidery unit and accessories in a padded bag that's durable and waterproof with a reinforced wall structure. Select a bag with a large compartment that can hold your embroidery unit, hoops, fabric and computer supplies. I like bags that include extra zippered compartments both outside and inside, plus removable dividers. A bag with soft grip handles and a removable shoulder strap makes carrying it to class much more comfortable.

**Uses:**
Tote or store your embroidery unit and supplies in this safe sturdy case.

## Notions Tote Bag

**Features:**
Look for a durable exterior, padded interior and sturdy sides for a suitable notions tote. Some of these organizers include removable inserts with various pocket sizes. The bag shown measures about 11½" × 15" × 5" deep and may include an adjustable padded shoulder strap.

**Uses:**
This handy bag stores a wide assortment of notions and feet for your sewing machine or serger. The price is modest, and many people utilize more than one.

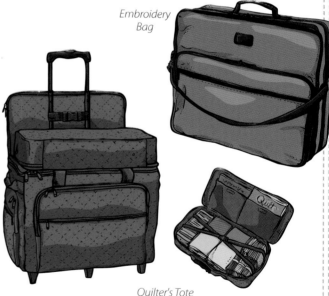

*Embroidery Bag*

*Quilter's Tote*

## NOTE from NANCY

I offered the first notions bag in my catalog in the early 1990s. We purchased it from a supplier for fishing equipment—it was originally designed for bait! I knew sewing enthusiasts would love all the pockets for small notion items. More than a decade later, a bag similar to that first notions bag is still available—and it's just as useful. Plus, it is definitely more stylish!

## Quilter's Tote

**Features:**
This large, zippered tote has plenty of pockets, plus a built-in pressing station with a 1" grid. It's great for storing quilting projects in progress. The zippered tote measures 20" × 28" with a 2" gusset for expansion.

**Uses:**
Use this tote to store your quilting projects and tools in one convenient place.

# 3
# Just for Quilting

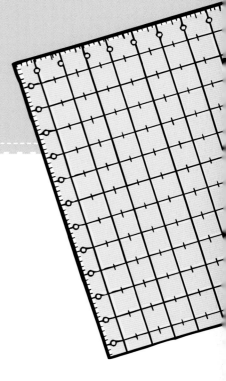

Quilting doesn't need to be intimidating! Start with the right tools and eliminate the pitfalls. You'll love these awesome quilting tools: From measuring to binding, your job is made easy and fun!

# ROTARY CUTTERS

When I first started quilting, there weren't many rotary cutters available. Now there is a plethora of cutters with a variety of blade sizes, handles, safety latches and colors. Choose the cutter that best suits your needs, and trim your cutting time in half!

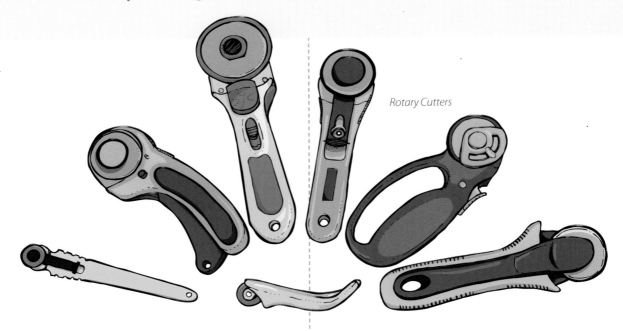

*Rotary Cutters*

## Rotary-Cutter Blades

Rotary-cutter blades range in size from 18mm–60mm. The smaller 18mm cutting blade is great for quilting and craft projects. It quickly cuts curves and tight places on a pattern. The 45mm cutter is the most essential cutter—the quilter's choice! It handles well, and the blade glides through many layers of cotton fabric. The 60mm cutter is the largest and is perfect for fabrics with loft such as fleece, felt and wool. A retractable blade with a safety lock for right- and left-handed use has become very popular with quilting enthusiasts. Replacement blades are available for each cutter, and decorative blades are available for 45mm cutters.

## Rotary-Cutter Handles

Choose a handle shape that feels comfortable to you—whether straight, curved, angled or weighted, everyone prefers something different. Color shouldn't be a *main* consideration, but it should be a bold enough color for easy visibility.

## Rotary-Cutter Safety Lock

If you have a household with a small child or curious pets, consider a cutter with a safety lock. The safety lock secures the blade when not in use and can lock the blade in an open or closed position.

## NOTE from NANCY

Speaking of safety, here are some good points to ponder.

- Retract and lock the blade every time you put the cutter down to avoid accidents. IT'S A GOOD HABIT!

- Take care when changing blades. You might even consider a cutter with a simple blade replacement feature.

- Always use a cutting mat and ruler designed for rotary cutting. Cutting mats are usually designed to self-heal when you cut on them, and regular rulers don't have a high enough lip for guiding the cutter.

- Do your cutting standing up for the best leverage. It is hard to hold a ruler or cutter when you are in a sitting position.

- Concentrate on what you are doing and cut with care. It's too easy to accidentally cut something you hadn't intended to cut when you are distracted.

Take good care of your rotary blades and you will reap a money-saving investment. The blade sharpener is for rotary blades only, but the tool cleaner and cutter glide work well for other cutting equipment and rubber stamps.

## Rotary Cutter Blade Sharpener

**Features:**

My favorite rotary cutter blade sharpener is an orbital sharpener that accommodates 45mm and 60mm blades. It includes two grinding wheels—one fine and one coarse. The safety cover keeps your fingers safe when sharpening.

**Uses:**

The orbital sharpener safely removes nicks and burrs from rotary blades and keeps them razor sharp. Sharpen blades for quilting, crafts, upholstery, paper cutting and more.

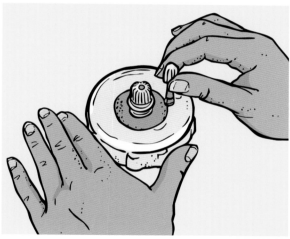

*Rotary-Blade Sharpener*

*Tool Cleaners*

## EZ Tool Cleaner and Cutter Glide

**Features:**

EZ Tool Cleaner is a liquid solution perfect for cleaning cutting and punching tools. Cutter Glide solution comes in a container similar to a bottle of nail polish with its own brush. It gives cutting equipment a better glide and reduces wear from friction. This durable coating is solvent free and environmentally friendly.

**Uses:**

Use the EZ Tool Cleaner to clean your scissors, cutting blades, rubber stamps, punches and more. Simply apply the tool cleaner with a paper towel. A small brush works well to apply the tool cleaner to rubber stamps. Use the Cutter Glide solution to give a better glide to cutting and punching tools. Apply with the applicator brush provided in the bottle and let dry.

Rotary-cutting rulers are designed with a perfect depth for guiding the edge of a rotary cutter. An accurate edge guide yields straight lines. The best size ruler for a project is determined by the blocks you cut. Obviously, a ruler that is the exact size of the block you are cutting is the handiest.

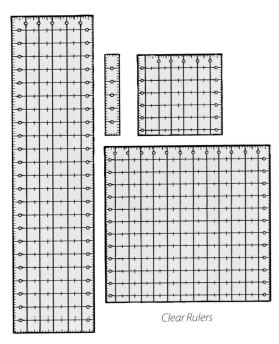

*Clear Rulers*

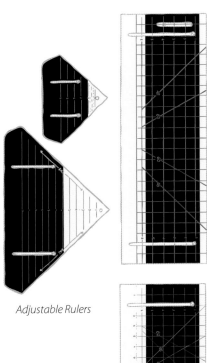

*Adjustable Rulers*

## Clear Rulers

### Features:

The most popular sizes of clear rulers for rotary cutting include 6" × 24", 4" × 12" and 15" square. Some rulers have lines for 30°, 45° and 60° angles printed on them, plus right- and left-hand numbering. Narrow ⅛" markings are not on all rulers, but they really come in handy. Buy a ruler that has markings visible over both light and dark fabrics. A nonslip backing is another nice feature. However, stick-on trims are available to create a nonslip surface for rulers.

### Uses:

Use clear rulers to measure and as an edge guide for rotary cutting. The 6" × 24" ruler works well for 44-45" fabric folded in half.

## NOTE from NANCY

There are many sizes of clear rulers available. The sizes mentioned above are my favorite for quilting and sewing.

## Adjustable Rulers

### Features:

Adjustable rulers include a fabric guide that slides to the desired measurement and is secured with two screws that hold the guide securely in place.

### Uses:

The innovative adjustable rulers make cutting patchwork pieces quick, easy and very precise. Repetitive cuts are accurate from start to finish.

If your rulers don't have adjustable fabric guides, simply mark them with tape for frequently used lines. Place the tape on the reverse side of the ruler. It saves time finding the correct line each time you make a cut. Fluorescent tape helps you spot the cutting lines easily to reduce your cutting time.

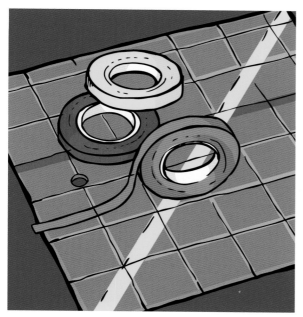

*Fluorescent Tape*

## Fluorescent Tape

**Features:**

Fluorescent tape is impossible to miss. I like Glo Line Tape. Not only is it transparent, this ¼" fluorescent-colored tape has a low tack so it doesn't leave a sticky residue. The tape is available in seven-yard rolls of day-glo pink, yellow and day-glo orange.

**Uses:**

Use fluorescent tape for highlighting lines and shapes on rulers. It is easily removed and can be repositioned for other dimensions. It can help make your rotary cutting simple and accurate.

## BUDGET FRIENDLY options

Masking and painter's tape are other options for marking your ruler, although they are not as colorful.

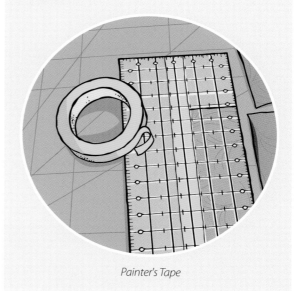

*Painter's Tape*

# RULER GRIPPER HANDLES

Pick up your rulers and move them more easily with a gripper handle. Holding the ruler with a gripper handle also helps keep the ruler from slipping and prevents cutting accidents.

## Ruler Gripper

**Features:**
Ruler grippers have lightweight, easy-to-grip handles and suction cups. They attach to most plastic or metal rulers with handy locks and release levers. Attach ruler grippers like the Gypsy Gripper to smaller rulers by using only one suction cup; the gripper is made of durable plastic, it is washable and waterproof, and the gripper handle works on most quilting rulers.

**Uses:**
Comfortably place and hold rulers exactly where you want them when cutting fabric.

*Ruler Gripper*

# CUTTING MATS

Cutting mats are a must-have when you are rotary cutting. Many people have tried to use cardboard and other household items, only to dull their cutter and make a mess in their cutting area. Use a mat to protect your cutting area and give your rotary blade the longest life possible. I have also included two of my favorite kinds of mat—the turnable mat and the mat with a pressing surface.

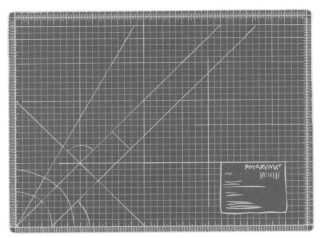
*Rotary Cutting Mat*

## Rotary Cutting Mat

**Features:**
Cutting mats come in a wide variety of sizes. The most popular size is 24" × 36", however the 18" × 24" is more portable. Cutting mats are usually marked on one side in 1" grids and may include 45° bias lines and 30°, 60° and 90° angle lines. Store your mats flat. Most cutting mats are sensitive to excessive heat and may warp if not in a flat position.

**Uses:**
A mat with a self-healing surface allows you to cut on either side with your rotary cutter. Cutting mats protect your work area and extend the life of your rotary-cutter blades.

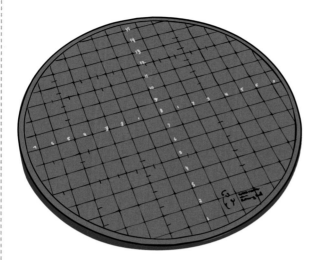

*Turnable Mat*

## Turnable Mat

**Features:**

The most popular sizes of turnable mats are 9"–17". Some have a ball-bearing base and rubberized feet, while others have a base that allows the mat to turn up to 360°. The self-healing cutting surface is gridded and marked with various angles for your convenience.

**Uses:**

The cutting mat turns up to 360° so you can easily cut squares, triangles and circles without turning your body.

### NOTE from NANCY

My favorite mat has a self-healing base that consists of three layers: a soft layer, a hard layer and another soft layer to prevent wear and tear on cutting blades. The mat is marked with ⅛" hash marks, ¼" gridlines and 1" grid marks.

## Press/Cut Mat

**Features:**

The hard-surface cutting side of these mats is weather safe and durable. The pressing surface is cushioned and gridded, allowing you to square as you press. Both sides of the mats have diagonal lines for quick and easy mitering. Several sizes of mats are available.

**Uses:**

Cut on one side of these mats and press on the other. Press/cut mats are great for taking to class!

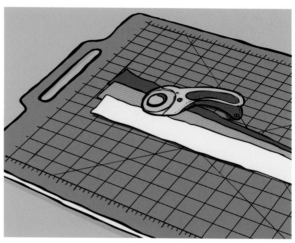

*Cutting Side of a Press/Cut Mat*

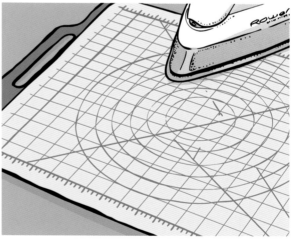

*Pressing Side of a Press/Cut Mat*

Half-square triangles or triangle squares are two equal triangles that can be sewn together to make a square—and quilters make a lot of them! Luckily, there are lots of tools to help us make them. Use one of the following suggestions to make half-square triangles quickly and accurately.

## Easy Angle

**Features:**
This 6½" clear acrylic ruler has black ½" markings and a built-in ¼" seam allowance.

**Uses:**
Cut half-square triangles in one step. The Easy Angle helps you cut half-square triangles to make squares without fabric waste. A ¼" seam allowance is included.

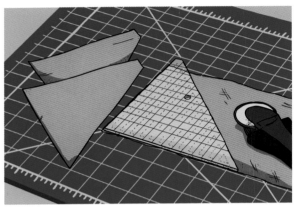

*Easy Angle*

## Sew Easy Guide Set

**Features:**
These transparent guides attach to the bottom of your presser foot to aid in sewing diagonal lines and ¼" patchwork quilting. Each guide has an adhesive area to attach to the presser foot, a center hole for the needle, a solid center line and ¼" lines. A set includes two guides—6¼" and 11¼".

**Uses:**
Use these stitching guides to sew diagonally from one corner of your block to the other without marking your fabric. The Sew Easy Guide Set is perfect for diagonal quilting.

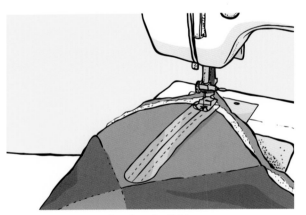

*Sew Easy Set Guide*

## Clearly Perfect Angles

**Features:**
The Clearly Perfect Angles template measures 8½" × 11" and is color coded for easy use. The template includes ¼" and ⅝" seam guides on each side of the center.

**Uses:**
This stitching guide helps you sew accurate 45° angles without paper, pencils or pins. The template clings easily to acrylic sewing tables and is always in position. It works great for triangle squares, flying geese, snowballs, miters, binding and more.

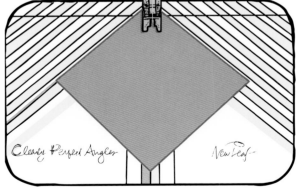

*Clearly Perfect Angles*

## Quick Quarter

**Features:**

These see-through plastic tools provide convenient, accurate marking guides when making half-square and quarter-square triangles from fabric squares. Two sizes are available: 8" and 12".

**Uses:**

Use this special tool to make triangle piecing fast and easy. Position the tool from corner to corner on a quilt square; mark. The outer lines are ¼" stitching guidelines, while the center slot is the cutting line.

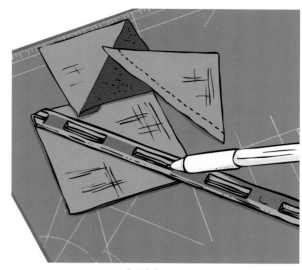

*Quick Quarter*

# ON-POINT TRIANGLE TOOLS

This no-math tool is ideal for cutting large triangles used for setting quilt blocks on point. It is designed to take the hassle out of cutting setting triangles. It folds open to cut large, accurate setting triangles while minimizing fabric scraps.

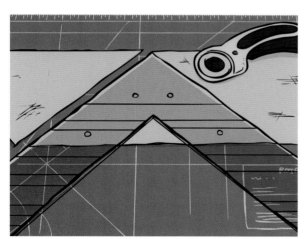

*Flip-n-Set*

## Flip-n-Set

**Features:**

My favorite ruler for setting triangles and blocks on point is the Flip-n-Set. It's easy to use, and *fun* to use! This heavy-duty acrylic tool measures 3" × 17⅞" and folds easily for storage. The Flip-n-Set identifies the correct strip size and provides accurate guidelines for cutting proportionate triangles.

**Uses:**

Cut accurate triangles quickly with no fuss and no math.

The Get Squared Ruler and the Block Marker Rulers are two of my favorite rulers for marking perfectly centered quilt blocks. You'll achieve accurate sizing with the Block Marker Rulers and be able to audition fussy-cut designs in the convenient center opening of the Get Squared Ruler.

## Get Squared Ruler

**Features:**
The Get Squared ruler is two acrylic square rulers in one—an 8½" outer square and a 4½" inner square. Each ruler has thick color-coded markings: black 1" lines, thin black ½" lines, teal ¼" lines and pink ⅛" dash lines. Teardrop cutouts accommodate the rotary-cutter blade when cutting the inner square. Both squares include ¼" seam allowances.

**Uses:**
The Get Squared ruler is wonderful for fussy cutting—no more marking or tracing. Audition designs using the center square opening. Then cut with your rotary cutter right to the corners using the unique teardrop opening.

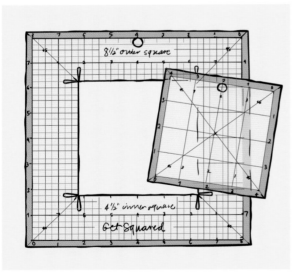

*Get Squared*

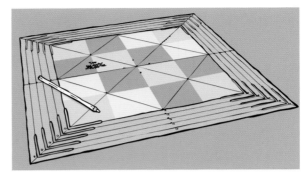

*Block Marker*

## Block Marker

**Features:**
The original Block Marker marks blocks 6"–17", and the Junior Block Marker marks blocks 6"–12". The center points of the Junior Block Marker are used for 3"–5" squares.

**Uses:**
Get perfectly centered quilt blocks without doing the math. By working from the center outward, you'll be able to make sure sides and corners of your blocks are perfectly aligned.

### NOTE from NANCY

No matter how hard I try, I can't make two quilt blocks the same size! When I first saw the Block Marker, I knew it was meant for me.

Plan your quilts and wall hangings by placing the blocks on a design wall before you start stitching them. You'll avoid tedious ripping, and you can view your color scheme before it's time for the finishing touches. A design wall also helps keep your blocks organized before stitching.

*Portable Design Wall*

## Portable Design Wall

**Features:**

Portable design walls are made to be assembled easily. Because they're portable, they break down to fit in your tote bag, though they often come with their own carrying bags. They are great to take to class, but are also handy for the space-deprived quilter and can be used instead of a full-scale design wall—and then conveniently broken down and tucked away. These are most commonly made from preshrunk cotton flannel, which holds the blocks better without pins than regular cotton, come in various sizes—from 36" × 36" to 72" × 72"—and weigh no more than 5 pounds when packed in its carrying case.

**Uses:**

Audition your quilt fabrics and your quilt layout before you start stitching. Fabric pieces stick to the white flannel—no pinning necessary! It's ideal for planning quilts and wall hangings.

## BUDGET FRIENDLY option

It's easy to make your own design wall and is much less expensive. Make a permanent design wall or a portable one you can take with you to class. My favorite design wall is made from fiberboard or stiff foam insulation and is covered with flannel fabric. If you are not able to find wide flannel, use a queen-size flannel sheet. Wrap the board and tape the flannel to the back side. Mount the flannel-wrapped board on your wall with screws. For a more portable wall, use a flannel-backed vinyl tablecloth. Tack it to your wall, and if you need to move it, simply roll it up with your blocks in place. The Internet is a valuable source to get other ideas—make your design wall today!

*Studio Design Wall*

# QUARTER-INCH MARKING TOOLS

Marking and sewing accurate ¼" seams is top priority for obtaining an even quilt top that fits together without a hitch.

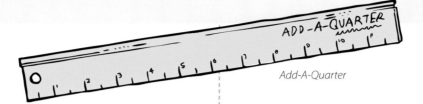

*Add-A-Quarter*

## Add-A-Quarter

**Features:**
The Add-A-Quarter ruler is transparent and has a specially designed ¼" lip on the length of the ruler. It's the only ruler like this that I've seen, and I love it. It's available in several sizes.

**Uses:**
The Add-A-Quarter ruler allows you to use your rotary cutter to obtain a straight cutting line or to quickly add an accurate ¼" seam allowance to quilt templates.

# STENCIL MARKING TOOLS

Stencils may be marked with a water- or air-soluble marking pens, but it is much easier to use a Quilt Pounce. Simply position a stencil on your project and wipe the powder-filled Quilt Pounce over the stencil—markings are complete and ready to quilt.

## Quilt Pounce

**Features:**
The Quilt Pounce looks like an eraser and has a large inner reservoir with a plastic lid to hold the chalk powder. The Ultimate Pounce Powder is high quality and nonstaining and comes in blue or white for marking on light or dark fabrics. The four-ounce bag is enough to mark several large quilts.

**Uses:**
A Quilt Pounce is the ultimate marking tool for stencils. The Ultimate Pounce Powder markings disappear with the heat of an iron.

*Quilt Pounce*

### BUDGET FRIENDLY option

Use a fine talcum powder or chalk and spread it over a perforated design or stencil with cotton batting. Or pounce using a fabric bag filled with chalk or powder. Avoid powders with perfume or oil in them, as they may stain your fabric. Years ago, ground cuttlefish bone was used for marking stencils.

Create perfect circles for appliqués, yo-yos and other quilting applications using any of the following tools.

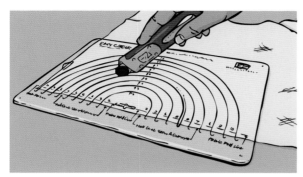

*Circle Template*

## Circle Template

**Features:**
Various templates are available for cutting circles, ranging in size from 1"–12". One variety has grooves in an acrylic template. An 18mm cutter fits into the grooves to cut smooth circles. Other templates are circular, and different sizes are nested into each other.

**Uses:**
Use an 18mm rotary cutter to cut circles from 1"–12" with easy-to-use acrylic templates, or mark circular designs.

*Rotary Circle Cutter*

## Rotary Circle Cutter

**Features:**
A rotary circle cutter is designed much like a compass with a cutting blade in place of a pencil. The handle design reduces wrist fatigue, and the cutter can be used right- or left-handed. The blade retracts, and the pivot spike often has a cover for safety. A cutting mat is necessary for use.

**Uses:**
Many rotary circle cutters cut $1\frac{7}{8}$" to $8\frac{1}{2}$" circles of fabric, paper, vinyl, film or leather.

## 5-in-1 Tool

**Features:**
This 6" tool takes the place of five different notions—a T-gauge, hem gauge, circle compass, buttonhole spacer and seam allowance gauge—so don't be surprised to find it in other areas of this book.

**Uses:**
Create perfect circles with the circle compass feature. Simply place the pivot point on paper and secure with a pin. Adjust the gauge to the radius of the circle (one half of the diameter or distance across the circle). Place a pencil in the hole on the adjustable arm of the compass to draw the circle. Cut out the circle template and place it on fabric to create a perfect fabric circle.

*5-in-1 Tool*

A beautiful binding with perfectly mitered corners is the finishing touch on an award-winning quilt. There are many tools to make binding your project easier—here are a few of my favorites.

## Binding Buddy Ruler

**Features:**

This 2½" x 30" acrylic ruler has two-color printing to make measuring and identification easy.

**Uses:**

Use this handy acrylic ruler to cut perfect 2½" x 30" bias or crossgrain binding strips without tedious measuring. Place the 45° bottom edge of the ruler on the fabric's edge and use your rotary cutter to create bias strips, or use the straight top edge of the ruler to cut crossgrain strips.

*Binding Buddy Ruler*

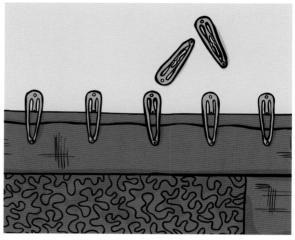

*Binding and Hem Clips*

## Binding and Hem Clips

**Features:**

These useful clips are made of rustproof, nickel-plated steel and are usually sold in a package of thirty.

**Uses:**

Binding and hem clips are used to hold quilt bindings and hems securely in place while stitching.

Pins and clips are essential for layering quilts. Size no. 1 curved basting pins are especially good for pinning quilt layers together. The tedious job of pinning is made easier with safety-pin covers and a tool like the Kwik Klip—they are definitely quilting notion must-haves! Large quilt clips are indispensable as well. Roll the quilt and then hold it in position with quilt clips.

*Kwik Klip*

*Quilt Clips*

## Kwik Klip

**Features:**

The Kwik Klip is a 5" long tool with a rounded, grooved brass tip and a hardwood handle.

**Uses:**

Close safety pins easily and effortlessly. Kwik Klip reduces quilt basting time, ends sore fingers and prevents broken fingernails. As the pin emerges from the fabric, allow the pin to ride in any groove on the Kwik Klip. Push the pin closure down and click the pin closed.

### BUDGET FRIENDLY option

Before I owned a Kwik Klip, I used a grapefruit spoon for closing my pins. The serrated edge on a grapefruit spoon works in a similar way to the edge on the Kwik Klip. However, the handle on the spoon is not quite as comfortable as the wood handle on the Kwik Klip.

## Quilt Clips

**Features:**

Several varieties of quilt clips are available. Jaws and Bicycle Clips are two of the most well known brands. Quilt clips may be metal or plastic, round or oval—it's all a matter of personal preference.

**Uses:**

Flexible machine quilting clips prevent quilts from unrolling while machine quilting.

## Safety-Pin Covers

**Features:**

These gripping covers, available in various colors, are designed to cover safety pins. The flat plastic top makes it easier to hold and close the pins.

**Uses:**

Safety-pin covers make your safety pins easier to grasp and maneuver, especially for those with arthritic hands and long fingernails. Pin your quilt in less time using these handy pin covers.

### NOTE from NANCY

Pair safety-pin covers with a Kwik Klip to open and close pins effortlessly. You will never want to close another safety pin without this handy duo!

*Safety-Pin Covers and Kwik Klip*

Stippling and meandering are basically the same—free-motion quilting using squiggly roaming lines to fill in a project area. The main difference is the distance between the lines. Stippling stitches are about ¼" between lines, and meandering stitches are farther apart. Lowered feed dogs, a darning foot and low-loft batting are three of the main considerations for best results. But I've come to love these other helpful tools to control the feed of fabric during free-motion quilting.

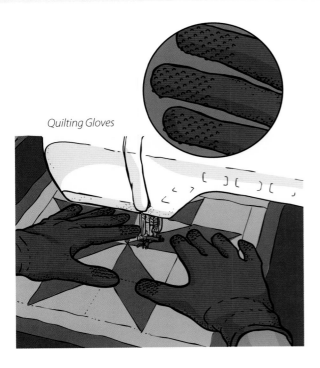

*Quilting Gloves*

## Lickity Grip

**Features:**
Lickity Grip is an acid-free, hypoallergenic, stainless and greaseless finger conditioner. It contains no perfumes or dyes.

**Uses:**
Lickity Grip conditions fingers for a better grip and control when rotary cutting, piecing, quilting and crafting.

*Lickity Grip*

## Quilting Gloves

**Features:**
Lightweight, knit, form-fitting quilting gloves have gripping nubs on the fingertips, tops and bottoms. Many are machine washable and dryable and are made of 95 percent nylon and 5 percent Spandex.

**Uses:**
Quilters love quilting gloves because they grip fabric securely to assure even movement when quilting. Plus, they reduce hand fatigue.

### BUDGET FRIENDLY option

Atlas Gloves, which are designed for gardening, work well for quilting, too. Or try the rubber fingertips found in office supply stores.

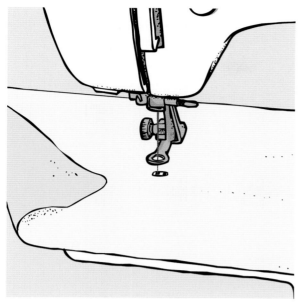

*Supreme Slider*

## Supreme Slider

**Features:**

The Supreme Slider is placed over the machine bed, with the tacky side down and the slippery side up. The tacky underside keeps the Supreme Slider in place on your machine, and the slippery Teflon surface stays in place without tape or adhesives. The 8" × 11" Supreme Slider features a center needle hole and can be cut to fit any machine.

**Uses:**

The Teflon top eliminates the drag of your fabric when free-motion quilting. The self-sticking bottom grips your machine and is easy to remove.

## Quilt Halo

**Features:**

The Quilt Halo looks like an embroidery hoop, but it has a tacky rubber surface that hugs your quilt tightly as you quilt.

**Uses:**

This tool sits on top of your fabric, and the rubbery edge keeps fabric taut with minimal pressure. It is easy on your hands—just slide your quilt around with the Quilt Halo on top of your basted quilt. Stitch an area, lift, reposition and continue stitching. Use gentle pressure on the Quilt Halo as you quilt.

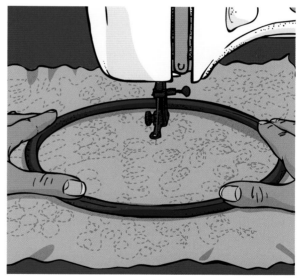

*Quilt Halo*

# 4
# Thread-Tale Tools

A creative project without thread is like a sewing machine without a needle. These tools will help you in your artistic endeavors that use thread and yarns by hand or machine.

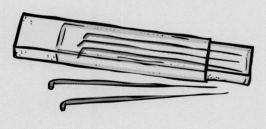

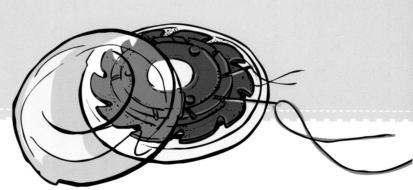

# THREAD GUIDES

Thread guides allow the thread to feed down to the needle without tangling. These are especially great for those problematic threads, like metallics, that really should feed into the machine with the spool in a vertical position. These tools help eliminate problems such as thread breakage, skipped and uneven stitches, thread pile-ups and more.

## Wonder Thread Guide

**Features:**

This plastic spool pin features a curled metal guide that holds your thread as the pin guides it into your machine. It is simply placed over your existing spool pin.

**Uses:**

The Wonder Thread Guide feeds thread from the center of the spool, eliminating tangling, twisting thread pile-ups and breakage. It works with metallic and "sliver" threads and works well with horizontal spool holders. It also accommodates tall spools of thread.

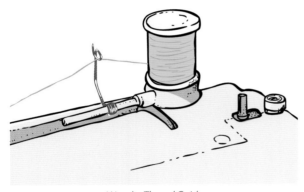

*Wonder Thread Guide*

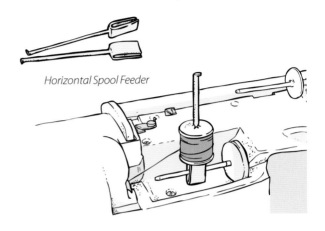

*Horizontal Spool Feeder*

## Spool Adaptor

**Features:**

Made of durable, lightweight plastic, these tools are designed to slip onto your sewing machine's existing spool pin. If your machine has a horizontal spool feeder, it will convert it to a vertical feeder.

**Uses:**

Some thread types do better when they unwind horizontally, and others when they unwind vertically. Spool feeder adaptors allow you adapt your machine to best suit the thread you are using.

### BUDGET FRIENDLY option

A vertical spool holder is a must for sewing with metallic thread—it will put an end to skipped stitches. If your machine doesn't have a vertical spool holder, you may be able to adapt the machine to hold the thread in a vertical position. Remove the cover from a rounded seam ripper (or use a short dowel or straw) and insert it into one of the holes on top of your machine.

Several thread stands are available for machine embroidery enthusiasts, holding anywhere from 10–102 spools of thread. Thread stands work well to organize all the threads for an embroidery project right at your machine. Most of the stands have a thread-feeding system that keeps your thread tangle-free and allows you to feed each spool of thread right from the stand. The 102-spool stand pictured is meant mainly for organizing, as it doesn't have thread guides like many of the other stands. However, it not only organizes your thread, but also holds hoops and stabilizers—an embroiderer's dream!

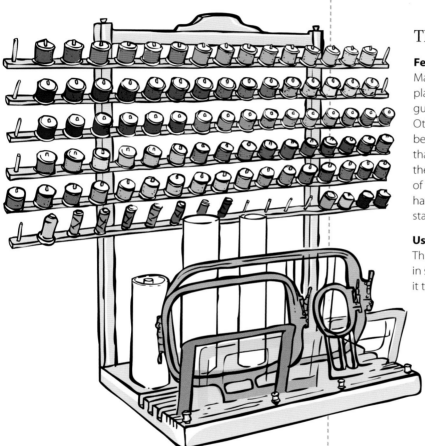

## Thread Stand

**Features:**

Many thread stands are made from a durable plastic and feature a weighted base, thread guides, rubber feet, spool trays and spindles. Others may feature a thread cutter or numbered thread pins for easy sequencing. Stands that allow you to feed the thread directly from the stand hold approximately 10–20 spools of thread in various sizes. Some thread stands have a platform for your machine, while others stand behind the machine.

**Uses:**

Thread stands help you organize your thread in sequence for machine embroidery and keep it tangle-free.

*Machine Embroidery Thread Stand*

# THREAD CONDITIONERS

Thread conditioners are waxlike substances used to coat hand sewing thread to keep it from tangling and knotting as you sew. Hands-down, the best brand out there is Thread Heaven. It has a patented formula to make thread more manageable and protect it from freezing, melting, UV rays, mold and mildew. Plus it's acid free and nontoxic. It uses static electricity to reduce tangling, knotting and thread drag. Thread Heaven doesn't stain the thread or fabric when laundered or ironed like many conditioners made of wax.

*Thread Conditioner*

## Thread Heaven

**Features:**

A small plastic box houses this amazing thread conditioner. Simply run your hand sewing thread over the conditioner in the open box to coat it with this magic formula!

**Uses:**

Thread Heaven reduces thread tangling and fraying and at the same time protects the integrity of the thread.

### BUDGET FRIENDLY option

Beeswax may be used to coat threads and keep them from tangling.

# EMBROIDERY CLIPPERS

Every embroiderer needs good-quality scissors or nippers for trimming thread tails and jump stitches. Double-curved scissors are the best for trimming in the hoop, but a pair of spring-action nippers is handy and causes less hand fatigue for random snipping. Fine sharp nippers or scissors are highly recommended for quick and precise trimming—a good investment for professional-looking embroidery!

*Curved Embroidery Scissors*

## Curved Embroidery Scissors

**Features:**

Double-curved scissors are ideal for embroidery, as the first curve reaches over the embroidery hoop, and the second brings the fine blade tips close to the fabric to snip the thread tails. Lightweight scissors with large finger holes are easy to handle and give excellent comfort and control. An extra-fine curved tip provides a precise, close cut. Some scissors come with a soft plastic storage case for protection.

**Uses:**

Use curved embroidery scissors for trimming craft and sewing threads or embroidery jump stitches. The curved blade trims close to the fabric.

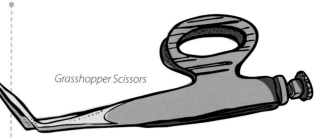

*Grasshopper Scissors*

*Spring Action Nippers*

## Spring Action Nippers

**Features:**

Lightweight nippers made of high-grade stainless steel are preferable. Curved blades are best for easy handling and cutting. A thread nippers promotes less hand fatigue than using regular scissors.

**Uses:**

Use all-purpose nippers for fine precision cutting. A gentle squeeze of a lightweight nippers snips whiskers and threads closely and precisely; plus, there are no finger holes for knuckles to get stuck in. Spring action nippers are a versatile and handy nippers for needlepoint, cross-stitch, and embroidery. The spring action makes cutting easy, even for arthritic fingers!

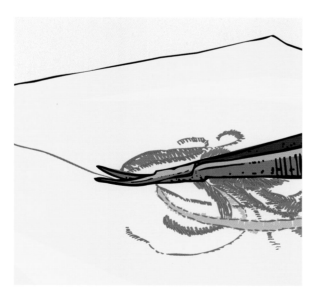

## Grasshopper Scissors

**Features:**

Here's another stainless steel, compact pair of scissors designed without finger holes (no getting stuck!). The tips of these scissors are very sharp and fine for accurate cuts. They're as cute as a bug! Pinch the wings of this 2 [³/₈]" scissors to cut threads with ease.

**Uses:**

Use these compact thread nippers for trimming threads on sewing and craft projects and for cutting jump stitches in machine embroidery.

If your needle breaks or falls out of your embroidery machine in the middle of your stitching, you may think all is lost. It would take forever to pick out all the embroidery stitches with a seam ripper! Now you can use a Stitch Eraser to clip the threads, and then whisk them away with a lint roller.

## Peggy's Stitch Eraser

### Features:
Peggy's Stitch Eraser is compact, rechargeable and cordless and has snap-on blades. The blades have been specially engineered to get under stitches, and then grab and clip them—without damaging the fabric.

### Uses:
The Stitch Eraser removes dense machine embroidery stitches with ease. Use it on the wrong side of the embroidery project to clip out the bobbin stitching. Turn embroidery to the right side to brush away the stitches.

### BUDGET FRIENDLY option

If you don't have a lint roller, use masking tape to lift thread clippings that have accumulated after erasing a stitch design with Peggy's Stitch Eraser.

*Peggy's Stitch Eraser*

A nostalgic rainbow thread braid is something I have traveled with since I first started my notions business. Instead of carrying twenty-nine different-colored spools of thread for quick repairs, I just pull the color I want from the braid.

*Thread Braid*

## Thread Braid

**Features:**

The thread braid features twenty-nine different-colored polyester threads. Each of the 348 threads is 27" long—the perfect length for mending or finishing a project.

**Uses:**

Use the thread braid for mending or decorative stitching by hand. Tuck a rainbow thread braid and a needle case into a repair kit for a college student.

# NEEDLE HOLDERS

Needle holders are especially important for handsewing needles that may be hard to thread and hard to identify. Package a needle case, a variety of threads or floss, needles and a needle threader (as shown on page 22) for a great gift!

## Dome Threaded Needle Case

**Features:**

This plastic dome case covers and neatly stores ten threaded needles.

**Uses:**

Store threaded needles with thread neatly wrapped inside the case. Retrieve needles easily and quickly, without tangles, from this great travel case that stores several pre-threaded needles.

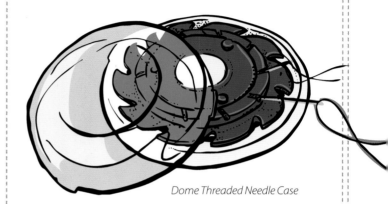

*Dome Threaded Needle Case*

### NOTE from NANCY

A friend once told me her granddaughter loved to thread needles for her and place them in this needle case. Grandma loved not having to look for her readers to thread a needle for quick repairs!

## Pebble Needle Case

**Features:**

Pebbles are designed exclusively for storage of John James needles. These color coded cases make it easy to identify the type of needle—such as chenille, quilting, beading, darners, embroidery, household, tapestry or sharps—stored inside. Each compact, snap closed pebble holds four to sixteen needles, depending on needle size.

**Uses:**

The pebbles are instantly visible and easily accessible in sewing boxes, craft bags, drawers and even handbags. Pebbles let you quickly identify the type of needle by the color of the pebble. These pebble needle cases are filled with my favorite needles, plus they're convenient, practical and stylish—stitchers love them!

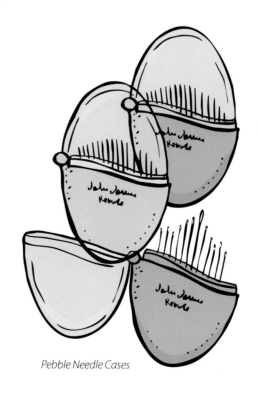

*Pebble Needle Cases*

## Magnetic Needle Case

**Features:**

This compact purse size magnetic needle case features a see-through plastic cover. The case may come with several needles.

**Uses:**

Store your needles in one convenient spot. The plastic cover allows you to see all of your needles at a glance.

*Magnetic Needle Case*

### BUDGET FRIENDLY option

Make an easy needle holder from fabric the size of a business card case with a snap or Velcro closure. Weave needles into the inner fabric to secure, or glue a magnetic strip inside the case.

# FELTING TOOLS

Use your favorite yarns and wool roving for needle felting. It's fun and very creative! Speedy needle felting machines with multiple needles are available, but simple hand tools are a fun and creative way to add beautiful texture and dimension.

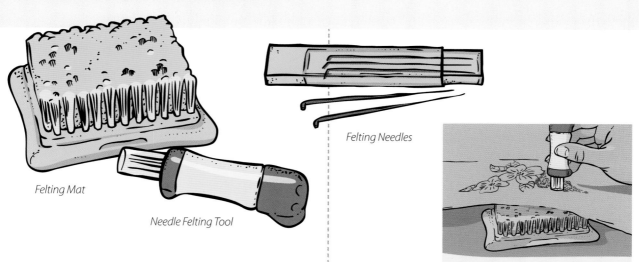

*Felting Mat*

*Needle Felting Tool*

*Felting Needles*

## Hand Needle Felting Tool

**Features:**

The needles used in the needle felting tool have barbed edges that interlace the woolen fibers as they are pierced through the fabric. The needle felting tool holds five of these barbed needles. Use a felting mat, such as a brush mat, under the fabric being felted to offer resistance to the multiple needles and to help prevent breakage while felting.

**Uses:**

Try felting designs on knit handiwork, sweaters and garments, wall hangings, throws, rugs and more. Suitable materials for felting include felt sheet with a minimum of 50 percent wool content, raw wool, wool yarn and woven wool fabric. Suitable materials for use as the base fabric include wool knit, woven wool fabric, felt sheet (acrylic and similar), woven or knitted cotton fabric. Add beautiful texture and a 3-dimensional appearance to both sides of a project by felting.

# 5
# Serger Sensations

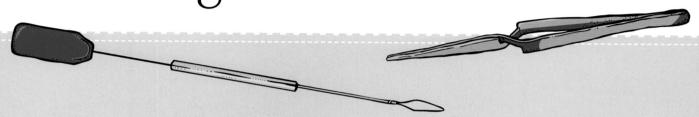

A serger stitches up to fifteen hundred stitches per minute, trims the fabric and overlocks the edge. This sensational machine is a real workhorse! The notions in this chapter help you tame the beast and make your serging experience more enjoyable.

# SERGER TWEEZERS

The task of threading your serger's needles and loopers is made easy with the help of serger tweezers. Tweezers also help you reach into parts of your serger with limited access space, enabling you to maneuver thread strands through guide openings and looper or needle eyes.

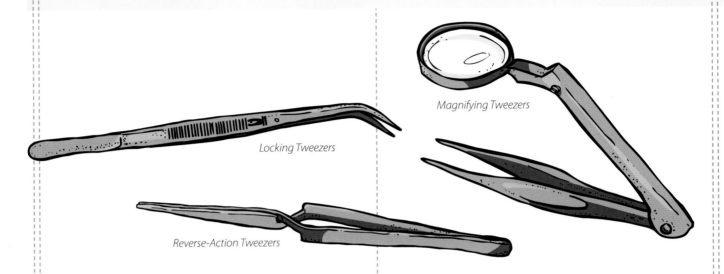

*Magnifying Tweezers*

*Locking Tweezers*

*Reverse-Action Tweezers*

## Locking Tweezers

**Features:**
Because this tool is used to grasp threads, it may feature serrated tips to hold the thread tightly and securely. A slight angle makes maneuvering easy, while an alignment pin keeps the tips together when grasping a needle or thread.

**Uses:**
Rethread needles and loopers with ease or use locking tweezers to aid in replacing needles. The bent tweezers conveniently lock in place when in use, for a secure grip.

## Reverse-Action Tweezers

**Features:**
The high-precision tips on these tweezers open when you squeeze and close when you release. These tweezers have straight tips and are smooth on the inside.

**Uses:**
Open these precision-control tweezers with one gentle motion, and then release to clasp around small parts, such as screws, when changing serger accessories. You'll find these tweezers easier to open and close than conventional tweezers.

## Magnifying Tweezers

**Features:**
These adjustable tweezers have a precision tip and 5X powerful glass magnifier. These handy tweezers measure about 4⅝" long, and the magnifier measures 1¼" in diameter.

**Uses:**
It's easier to see what you are trying to pick up with the handy magnifying glass on these tweezers!

With some sergers you almost have to stand on your head to thread the lower looper! The looper threader is a tool you can be very thankful for. It also works well for pulling the serger thread tail back through the stitches to secure a seam.

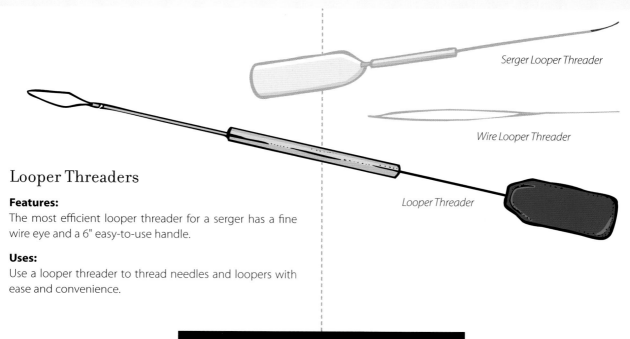

*Serger Looper Threader*

*Wire Looper Threader*

*Looper Threader*

## Looper Threaders

**Features:**
The most efficient looper threader for a serger has a fine wire eye and a 6" easy-to-use handle.

**Uses:**
Use a looper threader to thread needles and loopers with ease and convenience.

### BUDGET FRIENDLY option

Plastic dental-floss threaders work very well for threading your lower serger looper, and they are so economical! However, some are a little too thick for threading the serger needle.

*Dental Floss Threader*

# THREAD NETS

Yes, thread nets look strange—just like a hairnet for thread! But they really work to keep your thread from getting caught up while you are serging—a small price to pay for beautiful stitches!

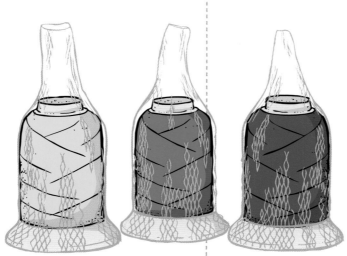

*Thread Nets*

## Thread Nets

**Features:**

Thread nets are usually made of a soft polyester netting. They come in many different lengths. The thread net should be several inches longer than the spool of thread with which it is used.

**Uses:**

A thread net protects thread from pooling and getting caught as you are stitching.

### BUDGET FRIENDLY option

The red netting used to bag small tomatoes in the grocery store, or cut-up nylons, work well for large cones of thread. Make sure to wash and dry them before using them on your serger.

## NOTE from NANCY

I prefer to insert the thread net in the hole at the bottom of the spool or cone and bring the remainder up over the spool to form a little thread basket. This is especially helpful for metallic and rayon thread, which are prone to pool at the bottom of the cone.

*Insert the thread net through the bottom of the spool.*

There's no backstitching on a serger, but it's easy to seal thread ends with seam sealant. Keep your serged seams from unraveling and avoid the time spent hand-weaving serged seam chains back into the fabric.

## Seam Sealants

### Features:

Fray Check and Fray Block are two popular seam sealants that work well for sealing serger thread ends. Seam sealants are generally a clear liquid in a glue-like container with a fine tip.

### Uses:

Seam sealants seal thread ends of serger tails to keep the seam from unraveling. These sealants dry clear but may become brittle if you use too much.

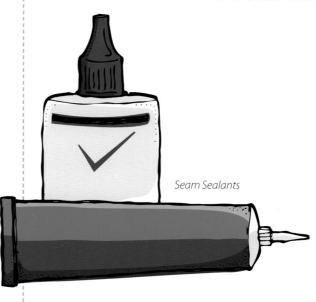

*Seam Sealants*

## NOTE from NANCY

To keep thread with sealant more pliable, place a small drop of seam sealant on a thread edge and place the seam on a folded piece of paper toweling. Touch the sealed edge with the tip of your iron, and the heat will dry the sealant almost immediately, forcing the excess into the paper towel.

*Apply a small drop of seam sealant to the thread end.*

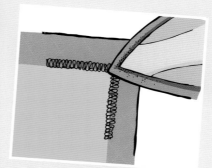

*Touch the sealed edge with the tip of an iron.*

# BOB 'N SERGE

Be budget-conscious: Wind several bobbins from one cone of thread and place them in the Bob 'n Serge. You'll be able to serge an adult T-shirt with the amount of thread on these bobbins. It's never been so easy to blend colorful threads in your loopers for decorative serging!

## Bob 'n Serge

**Features:**
Bob 'n Serge is a plastic bobbin holder that holds five bobbins wound with all-purpose or decorative thread. The hole adjusts to fit various thread spindles for three-, four- or five-thread sergers.

**Uses:**
Instead of using five full cones of thread for a small project, use a single cone and wind five bobbins using your conventional sewing machine. Load the bobbins on the Bob 'n Serge, thread the serger with those bobbins, and you're ready to serge. Use the Bob 'n Serge for thread blending on your conventional machine too.

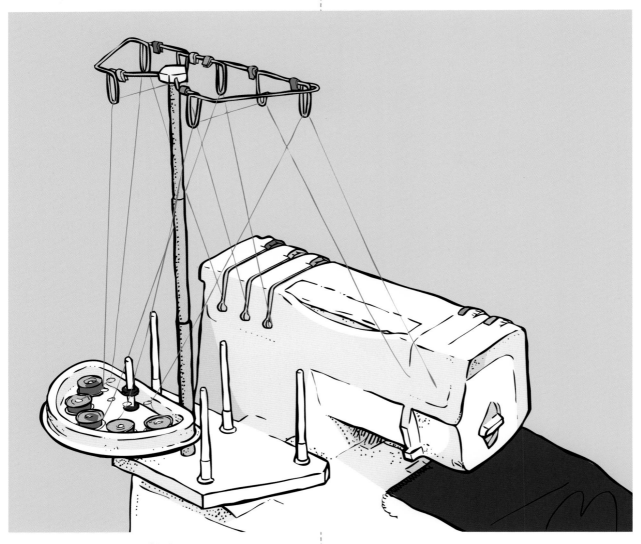

*Bob 'n Serge*

There are many seam rippers on the market, but my favorite rippers for serging are the surgical seam ripper and the seam ripper clipper. Both are able to remove seams quickly without ripping and pulling the fabric.

*Surgical Seam Ripper*

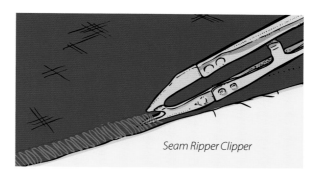

*Seam Ripper Clipper*

## Surgical Seam Ripper

**Features:**
Straight or serged stitches easily slide up the cutting edge of this razor-sharp ripper, while the curved blade protects fabric from accidental cuts. The wide plastic handle provides comfort, and a protective cap is included for the blade.

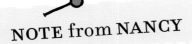

### NOTE from NANCY

Make sure your surgical seam ripper has a handle for extra leverage. If it doesn't have a handle, consider sandwiching and gluing the blade between two Popsicle sticks.

**Uses:**
Use this handy seam ripper to rip seams quickly without damaging the fabric.

## Seam Ripper Clipper

**Features:**
An advantage of a seam ripper clipper is that its angled nose can get into a seam and remove stitches without ripping the fabric. This spring action tool makes clipping easy and also eliminates hand fatigue. You'll wonder how you ever got along without this handy rip-it-and-clip-it tool!

**Uses:**
Use the seam ripper clipper to rip seams and clip thread tails with one tool.

### NOTE from NANCY

The seam ripper clipper is also featured on page 15. It is one of my favorite notions for both regular sewing and for serging.

### NOTE from NANCY

The easiest way to remove serger seams is to clip the threads at ½" intervals, then pull out the lower looper thread. Use an adhesive lint roller to pick up the excess thread clippings.

# SCRAP CATCHER

Sergers trim fabric and create quite an assortment of scraps and threads that usually end up on your serger table, your lap or the floor. Attach a scrap catcher, and you'll be able to spend less time cleaning and more time serging!

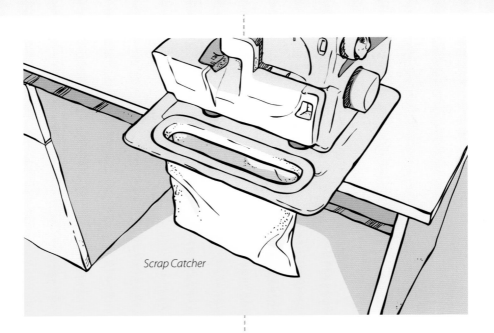

*Scrap Catcher*

## Scrap Catcher

**Features:**

This catch-all notion collects the trimmings in a handy bag that's easy to empty. Look for a scrap catcher with a foam pad (about 12" square) that fits snugly under your serger and absorbs vibration and sound.

**Uses:**

This handy caddy contains the mess at your serger, plus it keeps your serger from vibrating and wandering as you serge.

### BUDGET FRIENDLY option

Make your own fabric scrap catcher. There are several patterns available online, or you can create your own version. Cut a rubberized drawer liner to fit under your serger—it works great to hold it in place while you serge.

Keep your serger foot pedal in place with a serger foot pad, such as the Pedal-Sta II or the Neez-ez—two of my favorites!

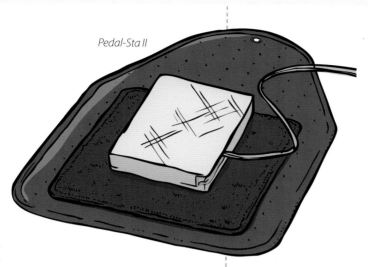

*Pedal-Sta II*

## Pedal-Sta II

**Features:**

This nonskid foot-pedal holder features a translucent vinyl pad with a cushioned pad on top.

**Uses:**

Keep your serger foot-control pedal from sliding and skidding along the floor as you serge. Simply fasten the included hook strips to the bottom of the pedal and then place it anywhere on the cushioned pad.

## Neez-ez

**Features:**

Position your serger or sewing machine foot control at a comfortable angle using this tilted pedal holder. An included nonslip pad keeps the base from moving as you're sewing/serging.

**Uses:**

Use the Neez-ez to keep your foot pedal from sliding around. The angled foot pedal helps relax your foot and align your body to improve your sewing/serging posture. Good posture wards off back and neck strain.

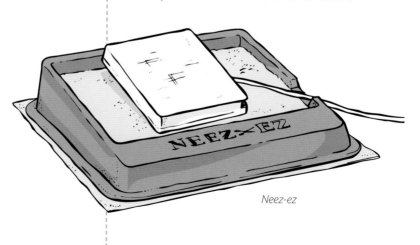

*Neez-ez*

Keep your serger clean and maintained, and you'll enjoy an ultimate serger sewing experience.

## Canned Air

**Features:**

Dust-Pro and Dust-Off are ozone-safe dusting sprays. They are 100 percent nonflammable and contain no chlorofluorocarbons (CFCs). These dusting sprays are often referred to as canned air. They contain a liquefied gas that acts as a propellant. The pressurized blast of air you get when using these products is actually gas vapors mixed with air.

**Uses:**

Use canned air to remove dust from your serger. Choose a product that is ozone friendly. *Please read the label for any precautionary information.*

*Canned Air*

These attachments make light work of cleaning up after your serger—inexpensive and ecofriendly.

## Mini Vacuum Attachments

**Features:**

These vacuum attachments are used with your full-power vacuum for optimum suction. They include a special adapter to attach to any vacuum hose, oval and round brushes, crevice tool and two extensions.

**Uses:**

Instead of blowing dirt and lint farther into crevices, use these attachments to clean your sewing machine, serger and computer keyboard.

*Mini Vacuum Attachments*

A brush for quick serger cleanups is an absolute must-have item.

*Serger Brush*

## Serger Brush

**Features:**

Use this long-handled brush to clean hard-to-reach areas of your serger and sewing machine.

**Uses:**

Clean lint and threads from your serger and sewing machine to keep them running in top condition.

### BUDGET FRIENDLY option

Keep cotton balls, cotton swabs and a good tweezers on hand for serger maintenance and cleaning.

# 6

# Sew, Press, Sew, Press

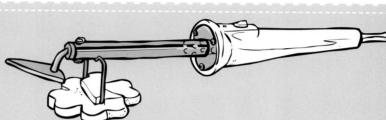

My late friend June Tailor would have loved this chapter! June designed unique pressing notions for sewing. She was very committed to finding the best pressing accessories, knowing that good pressing is essential to beautifully sewn projects. Times have changed, and yet many pressing notions have become timeless.

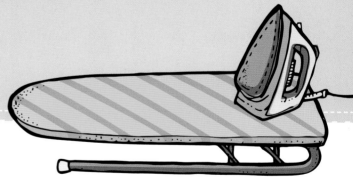

Choosing features on an iron is a matter of personal preference. However, if you're using the iron for sewing, quilting or crafting, pay close attention to the options that will help you get the best possible results for your projects. I especially enjoy using the following irons:

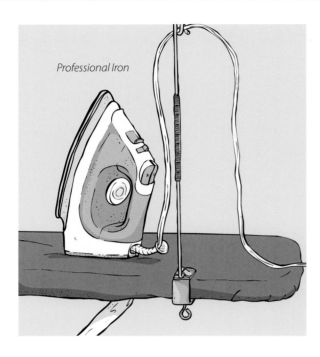

*Professional Iron*

## Professional Iron

### Features:
If you're looking for a professional iron, look for one with an oversized stainless steel soleplate that is scratch-resistant and has a nonstick finish. You'll want an iron that produces an exceptional amount of steam, uses regular tap water and has a variable steam control so that you can adjust from dry to high steam. Look for an antidrip system to prevent waterspots on clothing.

### Uses:
Use a powerful burst of steam for horizontal pressing, and if available, vertical steam for pressing hanging garments, drapes and fabrics. A hefty professional iron is perfect for pressing garments during and after construction.

## Steam Generator

### Features:
A good steam generator holds plenty of water. The tank on this iron holds more than a quart of water—enough for 1½ hours of ironing. Water should be housed in the base, keeping the iron lightweight and easy to use. A long cord from tank to the iron is a great feature for steaming garments and drapes. Also, look for a longer power cord that can be plugged in just about anywhere.

### Uses:
Use the steam generator for continuous high-powered steam at the touch of a button, or use it as a dry iron. Vertical steam allows the iron to be used in an upright position as well.

*Steam Generator*

## NOTE from NANCY

I personally prefer an iron that does *not* have an auto shut-off for sewing. It seems that just when you need the iron most, it has turned itself off.

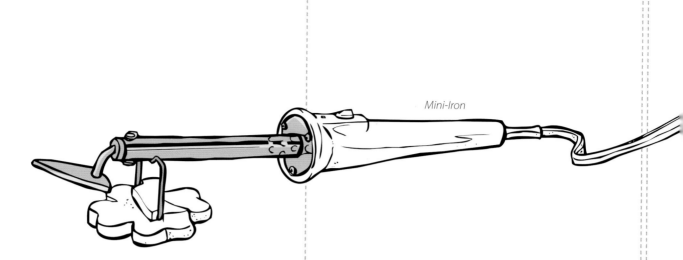

*Mini-Iron*

## Mini Irons

**Features:**

A good mini iron features a temperature control dial with settings from polyester to cotton. Its body should be light-weight.

**Uses:**

A compact mini iron is perfect for pressing quick bias, appliqués, seams and doll clothes and reaching into the smallest corners.

## Wooden Wedge Iron

**Features:**

Use a nifty wooden wedge iron for pressing cotton fabric. An angled head provides easy efficient pressing at your sewing machine.

**Uses:**

A wooden wedge iron is definitely a nontraditional iron—no electricity required! Use this tool for pressing seams open, to one side, or to crease fabric instead of using your fingernail or a traditional iron. Use it for appliqué, paper piecing, quilting and paper folding crafts. Eliminate a bulky iron for those quick-pressing needs.

*Wooden Wedge Iron*

# PRESSING SURFACES

Regular full-size ironing boards are available at your local hardware or big-box store; however, quality varies. Look for an ironing board that is sturdy, adjusts to various heights with ease, has a gridded top that allows steam to escape and has a cotton cover with an ample amount of padding. The following recommendations are for a pressing surface in addition to a regular ironing board, depending on the type of sewing you do.

## Original Big Board

**Features:**

The Big Board is a ½" thick unfinished wood board, with side rails that keep the board in place on your standard ironing board. A ⅛" thick needle-punch polyester pad and a 100 percent cotton cover with elastic drawstring are included with the Big Board.

**Uses:**

Iron with ease on this large pressing surface or throw a tablecloth over it to use as a buffet or dessert table during the holidays. Lower your ironing board to sit down and work for hours on any craft project. It is wonderful for quilting and to press large projects for home decorating.

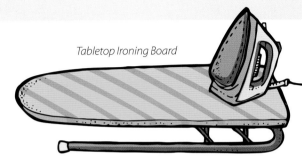

*Tabletop Ironing Board*

## Tabletop Ironing Board

**Features:**

This small version of an ironing board folds for storage.

**Uses:**

Use a tabletop ironing board in a small apartment or dorm where you have a limited amount of space or when you are working on small projects that fit on the smaller surface. Look for the same features as you would for a regular-sized ironing board.

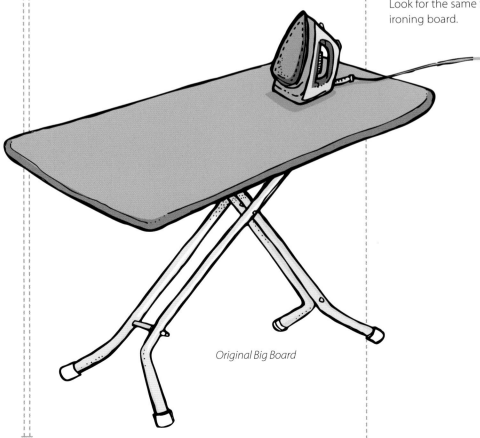

*Original Big Board*

## Portable Pressing Mat

**Features:**

A steam-repellent silver surface on many pressing mats is ideal for pressing cottons. Look for a reverse foam surface that will not scorch and can be used for pressing silk and delicate fabrics. Many mats include a vapor barrier in the center to prevent steam from penetrating the surface underneath.

**Uses:**

A pressing mat is convenient when an ironing board is unavailable. You can use the mats to safely iron on any surface—even on a floor or tabletop. Pack an ironing blanket in your suitcase when you go on vacation or travel for business and when you need an ironing surface in class.

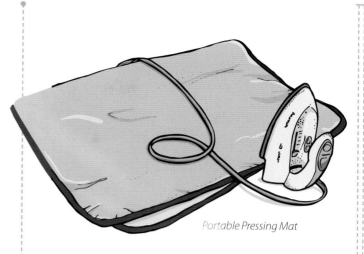

*Portable Pressing Mat*

## IRONING SPRAY

Starch used to be the premier product for pressing to give a lifeless garment some crispness, but now there are starch alternatives on the market that allow you to customize the amount of stiffness without starchy build-up.

## Starch Alternative

**Features:**

Starch alternatives are often found in nonaerosol spray bottles. Mary Ellen's Best Press is my personal favorite clear starch alternative. This ecofriendly spray takes the place of regular spray starch and leaves no residue; plus, it has a fresh lavender scent.

**Uses:**

Use a starch alternative as a stabilizer to customize the amount of stiffness desired—and give fabric a crisp new finish. Use for sheer and delicate fabrics or most washable fabrics that need a bit more stability.

*Starch Alternative*

# FABRIC PRESS CLOTH

Sometimes it takes a scorched or ruined project to help you learn the value of a press cloth.

## Fabric Press Cloth

**Features:**

Use a lightweight cotton cloth to protect your fabric while pressing. Use it with a steam or dry iron. Some are translucent, like the EZE-View Press Cloth, so you can view the fabric beneath.

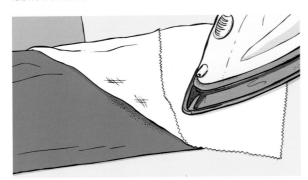

*Fabric Press Cloth*

**Uses:**

A press cloth prevents shine and absorbs steam moisture before it gets to your fabric. For extra steaming power, dampen the press cloth with a sprayer or sponge.

### BUDGET FRIENDLY option

Make your own press cloths by cutting a ½ yard piece of cotton muslin or broadcloth down the centerfold and finishing the edges with pinking shears. If you want a see-through press cloth, cotton batiste works well.

# APPLIQUÉ PRESSING SHEET

Your ironing-board cover will stay clean longer when you use a Teflon pressing sheet as you press fusible web to appliqué fabric. This eliminates getting that sticky residue on your board cover, which can accidentally transfer to other projects and clothing while pressing.

## Appliqué Pressing Sheet

**Features:**

A Teflon appliqué pressing sheet is transparent, reusable and heat safe. Use a dry iron because the steam doesn't penetrate the Teflon sheet. The press sheet comes in various sizes, but the one most used is an 11½" × 18" sheet.

**Uses:**

An appliqué press sheet eliminates sticky residue on your iron. It's ideal when bonding fusible web to fabrics. Fusible web easily peels off a press sheet, yet the web bonds tightly to fabric. Use an appliqué press sheet to preassemble multisection appliqués before fusing the appliqué to a project. This sheet also works well to protect surfaces used for hot-gluing projects. When excess hot glue cools, it peels off the sheet with ease.

*Appliqué Pressing Sheet*

Great pressing starts with great tools! The correct combination of heat, moisture and pressure smooths out wrinkles and sets the stitches. Since pressing is so vital to sewing, and garments have such unusual shapes like sleeves, collars, etc., it's no surprise that there are so many different specialized pressing boards out there.

## Tailor Board

**Features:**

The tailor board I prefer has three pressing surfaces for shaping various areas such as sleeves, darts and seams. Pads are usually included for pressing and shaping soft curved areas.

**Uses:**

Use multiple pressing areas on a tailor board unpadded for pressing crisp sharp edges, or add pads for shaping curves. A tailor board is a must-have notion for anyone interested in making beautifully tailored garments.

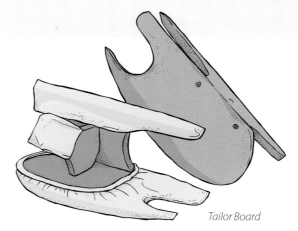

*Tailor Board*

## Point Presser and Clapper

**Features:**

The point presser and clapper is very similar to the tailor board, except it has the added feature of the clapper. No padding is available for the point presser.

**Uses:**

Use the clapper to flatten bulky facings, collar edges, pleats, buttonholes and creases. Use the point presser for pressing narrow, hard-to-reach seams of collars, belts, cuffs, corners and points.

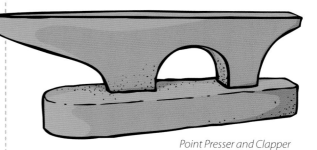

*Point Presser and Clapper*

## Seam Stick

**Features:**

A seam stick is a long, narrow wooden stick that is flat on one side and rounded on the other. It looks like a dowel cut down the center. The flat side keeps it from rolling as you press.

**Uses:**

Place a seam over the seam stick with the wrong side up. Press the seam open with the tip of the iron. The seam stick curves seam edges under as you press, which prevents seam ridges from forming on the right side of the fabric. A seam stick also works well for top-pressing a seam. Place the seam right-side up over the seam stick and press, using a press cloth, or add a fabric cover to the seam stick to prevent shine on your fabric.

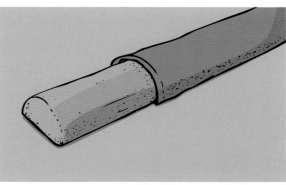

*Seam Stick*

# PADDED PRESSING NOTIONS

Use these specialty pressing notions on curved seams and other curved areas for easy pressing and a professional look. Well-tailored garments are well-pressed. Believe it or not, pressing makes your sewing look better!

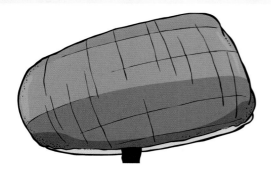

*Pressing Ham*

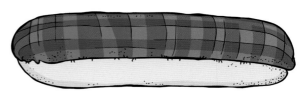

*Seam Roll*

## Pressing Ham

**Features:**

This ham-shaped pressing aid is usually stuffed with sawdust or foam. A pressing ham may be covered with wool on one side, for pressing fabrics requiring low to medium temperatures, and a cotton covering on the reverse side, for fabrics requiring medium to high temperatures. A pressing ham usually measures about 5" × 8".

**Uses:**

A pressing ham is used for pressing curved and hard-to-reach garment areas such as darts and princess seams.

## Seam Roll

**Features:**

A seam roll is approximately 4" wide and 11" long and made of cotton, wool or a combination of the two. It's a must for professionally pressed garments.

**Uses:**

The seam roll is a narrow pressing roll used for pressing seams to eliminate the seam imprints on the right side of the garment. It is also used for pressing sleeves, zipper plackets, small tucks and darts.

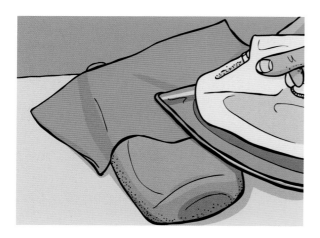

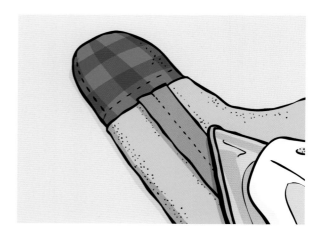

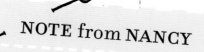

## NOTE from NANCY

During college I made my own seam roll using a tightly rolled magazine I covered with wool. After many years of use, it became lopsided. Before tossing it, I took it apart and smiled as I reflected on the styles found in the 1971 issue of *Vogue Patterns* magazine.

### BUDGET FRIENDLY option

Make your own seam roll using a magazine. 1) Roll a large magazine or two into a 3"–4" roll. 2) Wrap the roll with masking tape in several areas to hold it in place. 3) Cut muslin or wool fabric approximately 6" longer than the magazine and wide enough to wrap around the magazine several times. 4) Wrap fabric around the magazine, fold under the raw edge and pin in place. 5) Tuck fabric into each end of the roll. 6) Hand-stitch the folded edge in place.

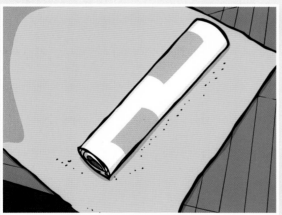

*Roll and tape a magazine.*
*Cut wool or muslin large enough to wrap.*

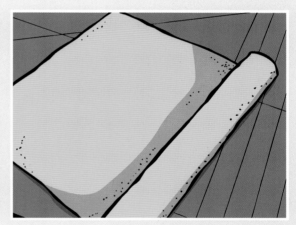

*Roll up the fabric.*

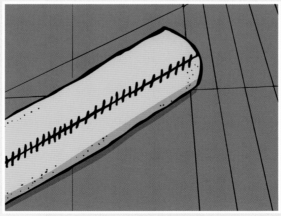

*Pin the raw edge under. Hand-stitch in place.*

# 7

# One-Task Wonders

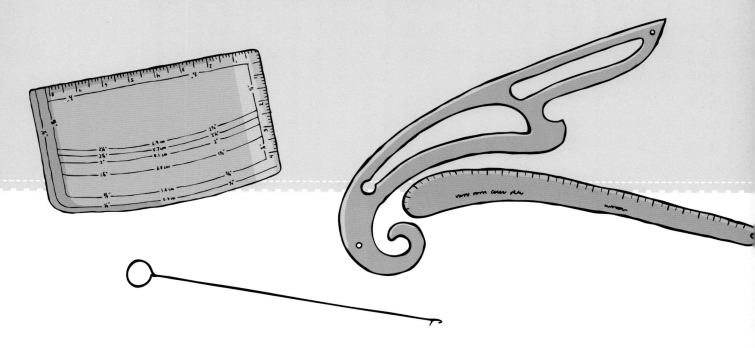

There are many sewing notions that do only *one* job but do it *very well*. The focus for this chapter is on those one-task wonders you wouldn't want to be without.

When you need matching bias binding for that special project, make your own. It's easy when you use bias-tape makers that fold the bias as you press. Slip the bias strip in one end of the tape maker and pull the handle as you press. It's that easy! The edges are always uniform the first time through. There are also fusible bias-tape makers available for those unique stained-glass-looking projects.

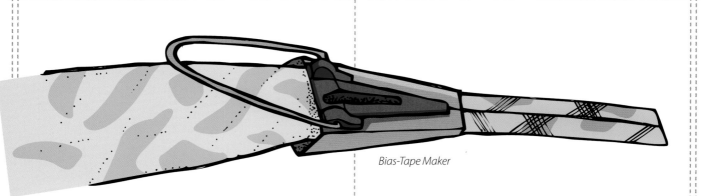

*Bias-Tape Maker*

## Bias-Tape Maker

**Features:**

Numerous sizes of bias-tape makers are available, including ¼", ½", ¾", 1" and 2". Plus, there are two sizes of fusible bias-tape makers: ¼" and ½". Each of the fusible bias-tape makers usually comes with a 13 yard roll of fusible tape.

**Uses:**

A ¼" bias-tape maker is perfect for lingerie straps and miniature projects. Use a ½" size for crafts and belt loops, a versatile ¾" for crafts and sewing, a 1" for garments and a 2" for blanket bindings.

Get perfectly shaped pockets every time using this simple tool! I have been using the Pocket Curve Template for many years. The original instructions were in Japanese, and the pocket template was used for shaping the curved areas on the sleeves and hems of kimonos. I wrote the first instructions in English to use the tool for making curved pocket hems.

## Pocket Curve Template

**Features:**

This ingenious metal template has four different corner curves. Use the side that has the best curve for your pocket. Two side clips hold the fabric in place while you press to prevent burnt fingers.

**Uses:**

Use the pocket template to press perfectly even corner shapes on your pockets quickly and safely. Simply form the pocket around the template, fasten the corners and sides with the clips provided, and press.

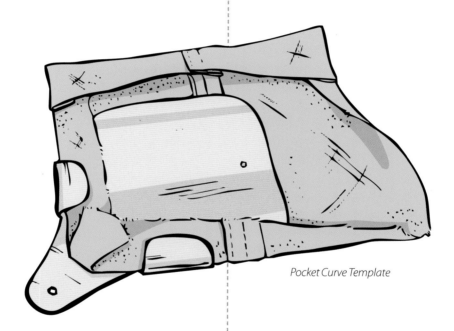

*Pocket Curve Template*

# BODKINS

The variety and uses for bodkins are quite limitless. The following are my favorite bodkins and what I like to use them for. Choose what works best for you and your project.

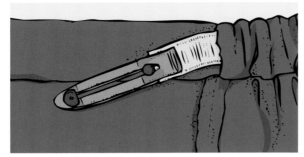

*Pincher-Type Bodkin*

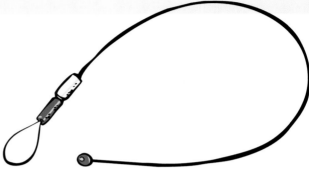

*Flexible Bodkin*

## Pincher-Type Bodkin

**Features:**

The metal teeth on pincher bodkins grab trim or elastic and hold it firmly until you release the sliding lock.

**Uses:**

Use these handy bodkins for threading elastic or trim through casings. Use three of the smaller bodkins to thread three rows of elastic in parallel casings simultaneously for even alignment, or use the wide bodkin for one row of wider elastic.

### BUDGET FRIENDLY option

Safety pins work for threading elastic and trim through a casing in a pinch, but it is much more efficient to use a longer bodkin with a sliding lock.

## Flexible Bodkin

**Features:**

This type of bodkin looks like a circular knitting needle. The moveable bead on the looped end helps secure the cording or trim so it doesn't unthread as it moves through the casing. The extra long steel cable is twisted to prevent kinking.

**Uses:**

Use long, flexible bodkins for inserting cording or trim through narrow circular casings such as gift bags and athletic wear.

*Ballpoint Bodkin*

## Ballpoint Bodkin

**Features:**

This type of metal bodkin measures about 6" long. The rounded ballpoint end is designed to push fabric without catching or tearing, and the eye of the bodkin is perfect for threading ribbon or narrow elastic through a casing.

**Uses:**

A ballpoint bodkin is especially nice to use for weaving ribbon. Simply insert the ribbon into the eye of the bodkin and use the ballpoint end to weave the ribbon through trim or eyelets. This cleverly designed tool is also used for turning bias tubing and inserting elastic into casings.

This expandable gauge divides an area into equal segments. Use it to measure equal distances apart, as well as the length of buttonholes.

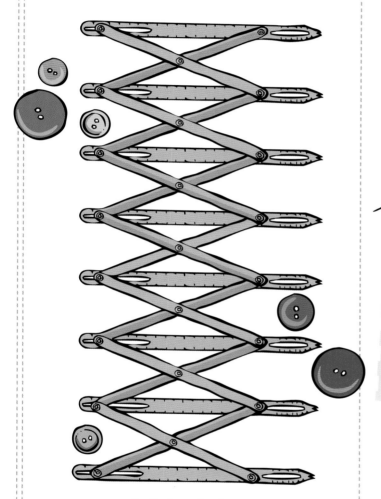

*SimFlex Expanding Gauge*

## SimFlex Expanding Gauge

**Features:**

This accordion style, metal gauge is very flexible. It expands to approximately 24" for correct spacing and placement marking.

**Uses:**

The SimFlex Gauge was designed for spacing buttons, buttonholes, pleats and more quickly and accurately. Easily mark horizontal buttonholes in the openings provided; the notch point measures the correct distance between the buttonhole and the edge of the placket.

### NOTE from NANCY

Whoever thought notions from your sewing room would also be useful in your kitchen? The SimFlex Expanding Gauge also works well to mark and equally space bars or cake for cutting. Spread the gauge so the distance between the pointed edges is equal. Poke pointed edges of the gauge into the bars or cake at the side of the pan to mark; cut using marks as a guide. Make sure to clean the gauge before using it again on fabric.

While definitely not a must-have notion, the pattern notcher is surely a one-task wonder! If you do any amount of sewing and have clipped markings for notches, you'll appreciate the amount of time this scissors-like notcher saves.

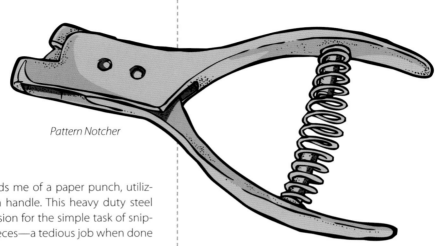

*Pattern Notcher*

**Features:**

The pattern notcher reminds me of a paper punch, utilizing the same spring-action handle. This heavy duty steel notion is crafted with precision for the simple task of snipping notches on pattern pieces—a tedious job when done with a scissors!

**Uses:**

Use this clever tool to snip ¹⁄₁₆" × ¼" slits in your fabric pattern pieces to mark notches used for placement. It isn't necessary to cut around triangular notches any longer with this one-step marking method!

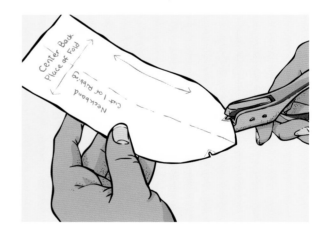

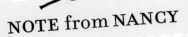

## NOTE from NANCY

I especially like to use a pattern notcher for seams or edges that will be serged. A simple nip may be hard to see, but the small notch made by the pattern notcher is perfect for matching serged seams.

These cutters are designed exclusively for cutting multiple layers of fabric to create chenille. Layer the fabric, sew in straight, concentric or curved lines, and then cut the fabric between the seams. Guide the plastic arm next to the bottom layer to prevent that layer from being cut. Then wash and machine-dry the fabric to bring out the soft, fluffy finish.

**Features:**

There are several versions of chenille cutters available. One type of chenille cutter has guides for four channel widths: ⅛", ¼", ⅜" and ½". Turn the dial to expose one of the 24 sharp blade edges. Made from high-quality tungsten carbide tool steel, this special blade can cut multiple layers as well as paper, cardstock, photographs, felt and fleece. The blade is not exposed, for safety reasons. This cutter works for both right- and left-handed users. Use it to cut curved and straight lines. Another version of the chenille cutter uses a 28mm rotary blade and has attachments for curved and straight cutting.

**Uses:**

Easily make your own chenille fabric.

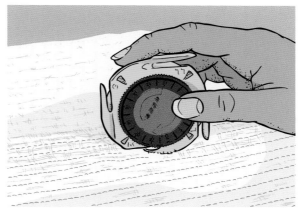

*Chenille Cutter*

A portable bobbin winder does one thing, but does it *very* well! No more unthreading and rethreading your sewing machine to wind a bobbin.

## Portable Bobbin Winder

**Features:**

A bobbin winder is a freestanding, compact machine that runs on batteries or with the included A/C adapter to do exactly what the name implies: wind bobbins. The version I use, the Side Winder, measures 3½" × 5", and the plastic compact case opens to sport the bobbin winding mechanism. A newer version has a cone holder for larger spools and includes a telescoping thread guide. Check product information to determine if your bobbin is compatible with the winder.

**Uses:**

This ingenious device winds bobbins without having to unthread and rethread your sewing machine. You can even wind bobbins while you're watching television or riding in the car.

*Side Winder*

A light box is so handy for tracing. It sure beats waiting for a sunny day so you can place your fabric over a design taped to a window!

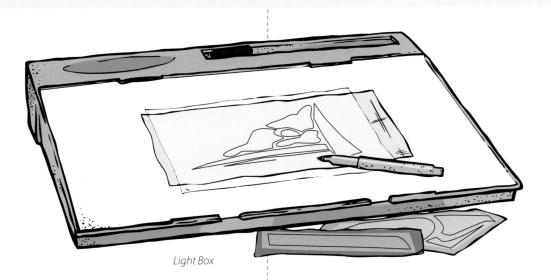

*Light Box*

## Light Box

### Features

A light box has a glass or plastic work surface placed over a color-balanced light source. The brand of light box I am most familiar with is LightTracer. The large LightTracer measures about 12" × 18", while the work surface on a smaller version measures about 10" × 12". Use whichever size suits your projects. However, the large LightTracer II has an ergonomically tilted work surface, and the entire space of the work area is filled with light, so there are no shadows to distort images. Static on top of either version holds your design paper in place. Some models have a handy recessed tray to store your drawing tools. The 7,500-hour, 15-watt fluorescent tube is easily accessible for changing. The small LightTracer has a 63" cord, while the large LightTracer II has a 72" cord.

### Uses:

Use a light box for tracing quilt designs and appliqué projects.

### BUDGET FRIENDLY option

A box, a fluorescent freestanding light, and a piece of glass can be fashioned into your own temporary light box.

These handy acrylic templates make mitering magic—with no math! The No-Math Miter Templates are easy to use: Just trace, cut, press, stitch and turn for quick double-mitered corners.

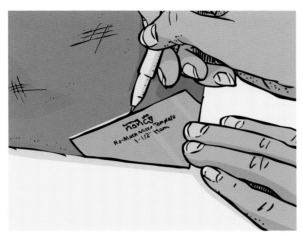

*Align the template in the corner and trace the cutting lines.*

## No-Math Miter Template Set

**Features:**

This set of six acrylic mitering templates can be used to miter corners on borders from ¾"–3" wide. This timesaving product includes a book with easy-to-follow instructions and seven projects.

**Uses:**

Create double mitered corners quickly with these handy templates. They are especially nice for mitering the corners on napkins, table runners, tablecloths, scarves, placemats and quilts.

### BUDGET FRIENDLY option

Clean finish backing fabric edges by following this process. Measure and make a mark that is twice the hem width from each side of the corners. Place transparent tape between the tape marks, extending the tape at each edge. Fold the corner to a point, right sides together, aligning the tape. Stitch from mark to mark, following the tape edge. Trim the seam and turn the corners right side out.

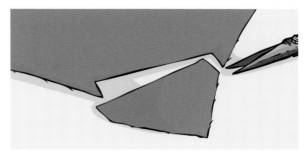

*Remove the template and carefully cut along the traced lines.*

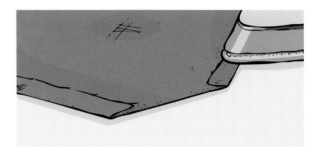

*Press up the seam allowances along the outer edge of the project.*

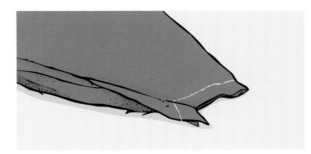

*Fold the corners in half diagonally, right sides together, and stitch.*

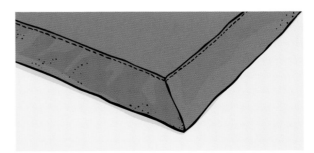

*Turn the corner right side out.*

Pick up pins, needles, metal bobbins and other metal items without having to stoop down to the floor. Simply extend the telescoping extension magnet and brush it along the surface of the floor. Gather your misplaced notions quickly and easily. The slim wand fits in many hard-to-reach areas for retrieval of metal notions and other belongings.

## Telescoping Extension Magnet

**Features:**
Some telescoping magnets extend to about 25" and hold three to five pounds. Many of these magnets have a convenient pocket clip.

**Uses:**
Use a telescoping magnet for picking up small metal objects such as pins, needles and bobbins in difficult-to-reach places.

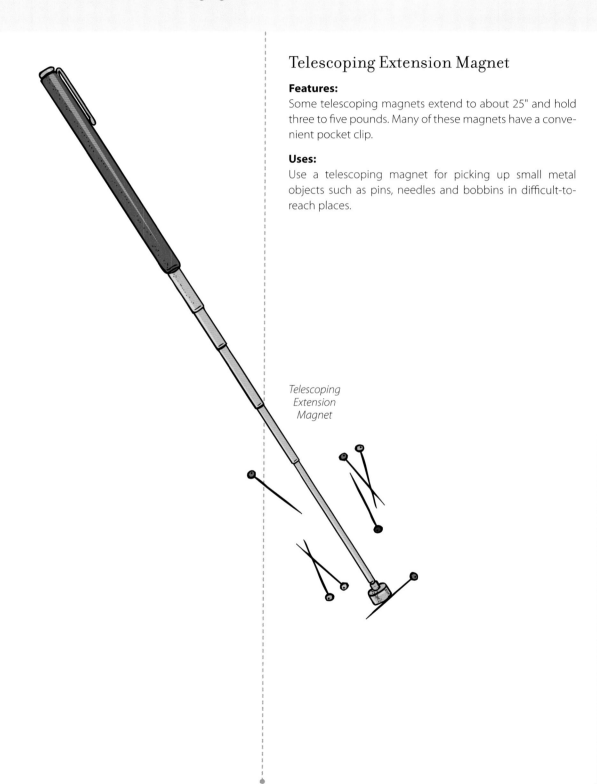

*Telescoping
Extension
Magnet*

Bling is definitely popular, and quality crystals and other embellishments with heat-activated backings are easily attached with an applicator wand specifically designed for them. My favorite wand is the Professional Touch Applicator Wand, as it is safe and quick to use. There are a variety of tips for different embellishments, and the wand doesn't require a stand to hold it each time you set it down.

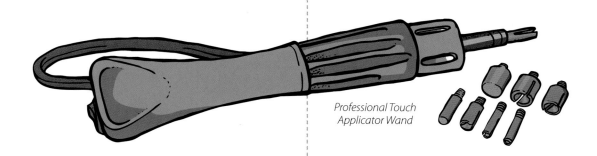

*Professional Touch Applicator Wand*

## Hot-Fix Applicator Wand

**Features:**

A good applicator wand features a short barrel for precise placement of hot-fix embellishments. It should feature a handy on-off switch on the handle, a long cord and a finger guard for protection from the hot metal barrel. Look for a balanced handle so the wand doesn't tip over when it's set aside. The Professional Touch comes with various interchangeable accessories for affixing different sizes and types of embellishments. The wand heats up and is ready to use in about two minutes!

**Uses:**

Easily apply hot-fix crystals, pearl studs, rhinestones and nail heads to almost any surface with an ergonomically designed applicator wand.

### BUDGET FRIENDLY option

Hot-fix embellishments may be attached with a hot, dry iron, but keeping them from shifting as you press is the biggest challenge.

I like to use the loop turner to turn small spaghetti-type straps. A standard loop turner paired with the Fasturn set are my favorite tube turners.

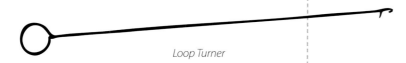

*Loop Turner*

## Loop Turner

**Features:**

A standard metal loop turner has a latch hook on one end and a pull ring at the other. The turner measures about 12" long.

**Uses:**

To turn a tube of fabric right-side-out, insert the hook end of the loop turner into the fabric tube and poke the hook through the fabric at the opposite end. Hold the pull ring gently while you pull the loop turner back through the fabric tube. Work with care so the hook stays connected to the fabric. Use a loop turner to turn loops ⅛" and wider with ease.

### BUDGET FRIENDLY option

Use an old-fashioned bobby pin to turn a narrow tube.

• Make a small slit in the tube close to the bottom.

• Insert one end of the bobby pin into the slit and adjust so the bend in the bobby pin catches the excess fabric.

• Poke the bobby pin through the tube, carefully guiding it so that the fabric doesn't come off the pin.

**Another budget-friendly turning option:**

If you serge a tube, simply thread the serger tail through the tube with a blunt or double-eyed needle to turn.

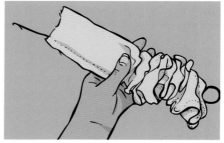

*Place the looper turner in the fabric tube, extending the hook through the top of the tube.*

*Catch the hook end of the loop turner on the top edge of the fabric tube.*

*Pull the loop turner back through the fabric tube, turning it right-side-out.*

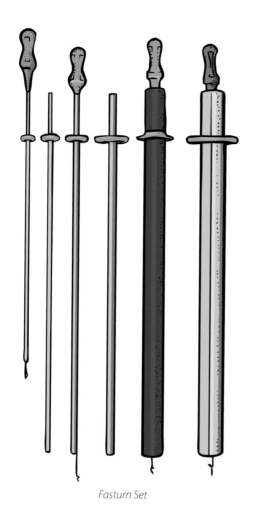

*Fasturn Set*

## Fasturn Set

### Features:

The original Fasturn Set comes with six brass tubes and three turning hooks. The tubes vary in size from ⅛" diameter to ¾" diameter. Larger sizes are also available, but the original set turns most common tube sizes.

### Uses:

Turn tubes from the smallest spaghetti straps to large upholstery piping with this set. There is a Fasturn in the set for almost any other tube I need to turn. You can even turn a tube and stuff it with cording at the same time. To add body or dimension to a tube, insert batting or cording as you turn the tube.

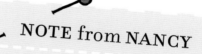

## NOTE from NANCY

When one of my colleague's son requested a magic show for his kindergarten class, she demonstrated turning a tube and stuffing it at the same time with the Fasturn. Believe me, adults are just as awestruck as the children watching this presentation!

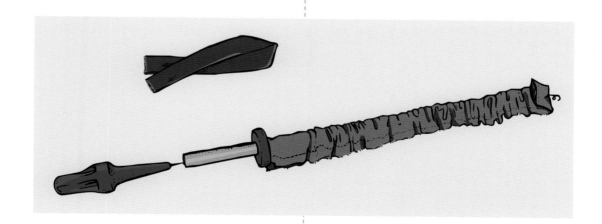

Copy or create any curved shape with this amazing flexible ruler. It holds a curved shape and allows you to trace and adjust it as needed.

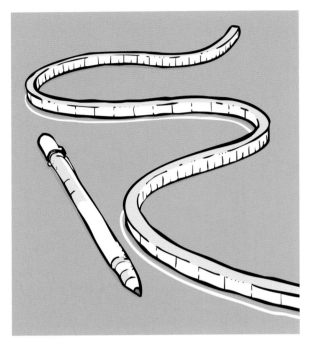

*Flexible Curve Ruler*

## Flexible Ruler

**Features:**

A good flexible ruler usually has a lead core construction; it's the secret that allows this ruler to retain its shape for accurate drawing. Most commonly 32" or 40" long, these rulers have measurements in metric and inches on both sides of the flexible tape.

**Uses:**

Use a flexible ruler to measure or copy the shape of curved areas on patterns such as the sleeve cap and necklines, or to determine the crotch depth on a pattern or garment.

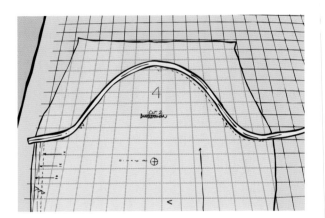

# FRENCH CURVE RULERS

French curve rulers or templates are perfect for quilters, designers, draftsmen and artists. They are used extensively by the garment industry for truing pattern lines. I especially like to use a French curve ruler to draw curved hiplines and smooth the curve of the armseye area after making alterations.

## French Curve Ruler

**Features:**

This flexible template ruler has several graduated curves and may be made of plastic, metal or wood. An aluminum ruler's curves will not chip or warp, but you will want to make sure the edges are not rough.

**Uses:**

Use a French curve ruler for designing, quilting and creating patterns. The most common use for this ruler in the sewing industry is for truing pattern lines.

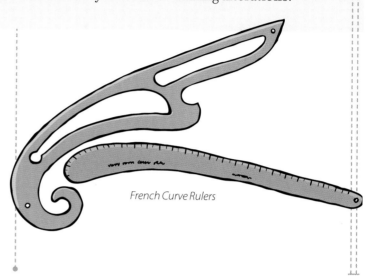

*French Curve Rulers*

# FASHION DESIGN KITS

If you draft, alter or fit your own patterns, this kit includes everything you need. Become a fashionista who creates classic styles with an impeccable fit.

## Fashion Design Kit

**Features:**

There are a variety of fashion design kits on the market, for a range of prices. My favorite kit includes a number of good rulers: a vary form curve, a curved stick, an L-square and a transparent graph ruler. It also comes with an informative instruction booklet, *Guide to Patternmaking*, which teaches how to use these tools.

**Uses:**

Drafting, altering and fitting patterns are a snap with the right notions. Home sewers, fashion students and tailors will definitely love a kit like this.

### BUDGET FRIENDLY option

The equipment in this kit can be found separately, but the savings is substantial when the essentials are bundled together. Treat yourself to the latest tools for a fashionably fitting wardrobe!

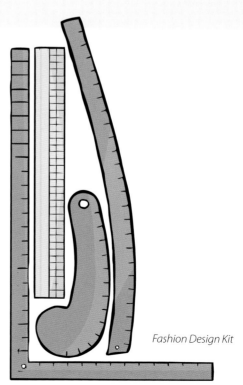

*Fashion Design Kit*

Mark your own hems using a handy hem marker. Adjust the marking ruler and simply squeeze the air bulb to release chalk as you mark a straight hem. This is especially helpful when your sewing buddy is on vacation!

## Hem Marker

**Features:**

Tripod-like feet keep a hem marker steady as you mark straight hemlines from the floor with a chalk line. Squeeze the air bulb to release ground-up chalk for marking.

**Uses:**

Easily mark straight hemlines on skirts up to 30" from the floor.

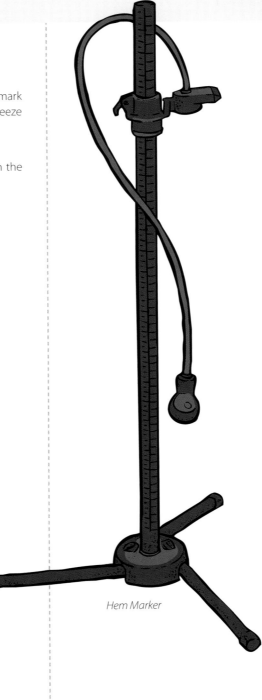

*Hem Marker*

Turn your hem up over a hem gauge to accurately measure the hem, then crease or press to get a crisp hem edge. Choose a metal or plastic hem gauge, depending on whether or not you plan to press up your hem with an iron. If you are using a plastic hem gauge, simply crease the hem edge with your fingers or a wooden wedge iron.

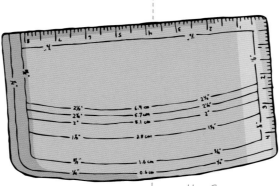

*Hem Gauge*

## Hem Gauge

**Features:**

Both metal and plastic hem gauges are available. I especially like the 5" × 9" aluminum Ezy-Hem Gauge, which includes both inch and metric measurements. The Ezy-Hem Gauge can make a straight hem from ¼"–4" and a curved hem from ¼"–2½".

**Uses:**

Use the right angles of a hem gauge on straight hems and the rounded end for curved hems. A hem gauge also works well for making shaped pockets, waistbands and belts. Press hems from the fold upward. Remember that a metal gauge is hot after pressing, so use care when handling it. Don't use an iron with a plastic hem gauge.

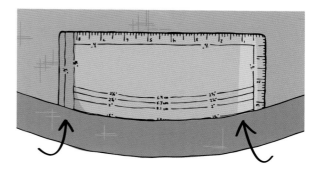

Sharp points on your pins and needles make your sewing task much easier. Unsightly snags and thread pulls result from burred pins and needles. Just a little maintenance keeps your pins sharp and ready to use.

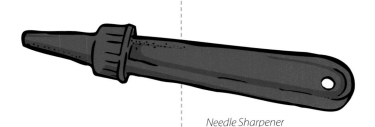

*Needle Sharpener*

## Needle Sharpener

**Features:**

The best needle sharpener I've found uses a state-of-the-art diamond sharpening stone to create a sharp needle point in seconds. The popular pink sharpener with plastic covering measures about 5" long. A round brass sharpener is also available, measuring about 1½" in diameter. The center of the round sharpener is a ½" nylon cushion that includes a polishing powder. Simply slide your needles and pins through it to maintain sharpness.

**Uses:**

Needle sharpeners are perfect for sharpening hand and machine needles and some pins.

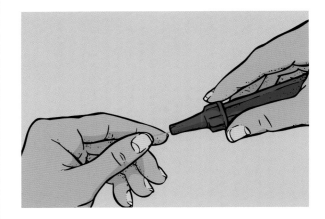

## NOTE from NANCY

Did you know the little strawberry that is attached to many pincushions is filled with a fine emery powder to sharpen your pins and needles? Just poke the tips of your pins and needles in and out several times to remove burrs and sharpen the tips

Celtic artwork involves a continuous interweaving of lines with no apparent beginning and no end representing the continuation of life. Quilters duplicate these designs with bias appliqué in highly contrasting fabrics. Steel pressing bars are the pressing bars of choice for most quilters, as they produce a very crisp edge, and steel withstands the heat from an iron for great pressing. Steel bars remain quite hot after pressing, so use care when handling.

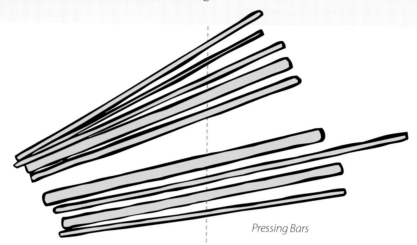

*Pressing Bars*

## Pressing Bars

**Features:**
The two most common materials used to make pressing bars are steel and plastic. Sizes available are ⅛", ¼", ½", ¾" and 1". The ¼" pressing bars are the most popular.

**Uses:**
Pressing bars are used to make bias for Celtic designs. The type of bias made with the pressing bars is very durable and suitable for use on clothing, wall hangings and quilts because of its tubular structure. It has a raised texture, which is lovely for Celtic or stained-glass designs.

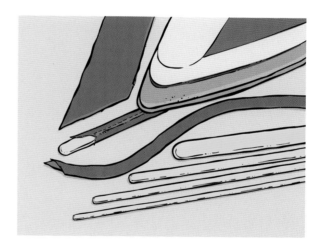

# 8
# Favorite Feet

Creative and time-saving feet are available for even the most basic sewing machines. No more frustration when satin stitching, binding, ruffling or stippling! Our chapter on favorite feet is sure to inspire you to give them a try.

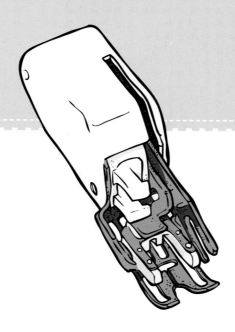

You'll be singing, "I can see clearly now," when you use this practical foot. Complete your appliqué stitching with ease and add trim using a double needle or fancy stitches—the open-toe foot helps you complete your projects quickly because you have full view of the stitches.

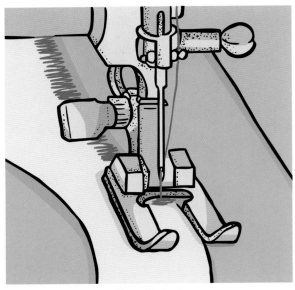

*Open-Toe Foot*

## Open-Toe Foot

**Features:**
The cutout front on this foot allows a clear view of the needle and stitches. You can actually see what you are stitching! The grooved underside allows stitches to pass easily beneath the foot so they don't get all bunched up. Some open-toe feet are plastic, and some are metal. Choose the foot that is right for your machine.

**Uses:**
You'll see your decorative stitches and satin appliqué stitches much better as you stitch. Also use an open-toe foot to bar tack by machine and to attach your favorite trim using a double needle. Or use it to stitch invisible machine appliqué with a blind hem stitch—it's wonderful!

## NOTE from NANCY

An open-toe foot is a must-have accessory and is available for just about every sewing machine. It is definitely worth the small investment because it is used for so many techniques such as appliqué, applying trim, double needle stitching and much more.

Use a ¼" quilting foot to stitch accurate ¼" seams with fluency. Guide the right edge of the foot along the cut edges of the seam as you stitch for precise ¼" seams every time.

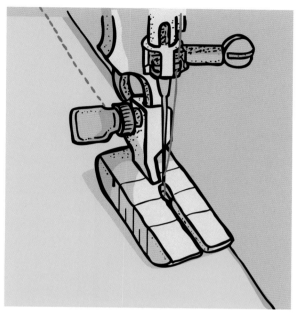

*The Little Foot*

## ¼" Quilting Foot

**Features:**

Although there are a variety of ¼" quilting feet on the market, I like to use the Little Foot because the right edge is a scant ¼" from the center needle position, so it's ideal for machine piecing. The wider left toe, a scant ⅜" from your needle, provides better fabric feed control—especially on newer machines with a wider distance between feed dogs. It also features ¼" notches in front of and behind the center needle position—perfect references for starting, stopping, and pivoting.

**Uses:**

The Little Foot is excellent for machine piecing quilts and any other sewing project that requires a precise ¼" or ⅜" seam. It is truly a quilter's delight!

*Note: To use the Little Foot, Bernina owners need a Bernina shank adapter for older models. To convert to high shank, use a hi-low adapter.*

### BUDGET FRIENDLY option 1

If you are able to change your needle position, move it to the right until the measurement from the needle to the right edge of your regular presser foot or zipper foot measures ¼".

### BUDGET FRIENDLY option 2

Place a lined 3" x 5" index card under the edge of the presser foot. The blue lines on the card are exactly ¼" apart, so you can adjust the position of your sewing machine needle using the card as a guide.

Make an overall design on your quilt top as you stitch through the top, backing and batting, moving the layers yourself as you stitch. The machine's feed dogs are down when using a free-motion foot, and you control the stitching. The Big Foot is my favorite foot to use for free-motion quilting. This giant free motion foot is designed to give more control as you quilt layers together, especially with stippling and echo stitching.

*Big Foot*

## Free-Motion Quilting Foot

**Features:**

There are several feet that can be used for free-motion quilting, and they may be made of metal or plastic. The shape and size of the foot may vary, but they are all used with the feed dogs of the machine in a "down" position or covered so the stitching is controlled by you. The large saucer-shaped base of a Big Foot provides more surface contact and helps keep the fabric flat without being taut. This foot is transparent to allow excellent visibility while you are stitching.

**Uses:**

A free-motion foot is especially helpful for stippling, echo stitching and landscape quilting. The Big Foot works especially well for echo quilting because the cut-out design in the center is ¼" from the needle, which allows you to create echo stitching that is a consistent distance apart.

A walking foot feeds the top layer of fabric at the same rate the feed dogs are feeding the bottom layer of fabric, keeping the layers even as they are joined. The feed dogs are in the normal "up" position. Don't let the looks of the walking foot scare you. It may look like a pretty complicated contraption, but it is really quite easy to use. Just attach the walking foot to your machine according to the instructions—then simply sew, and it does its magic! No more shifting fabric.

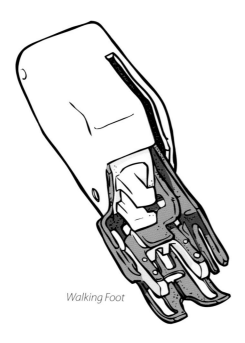

*Walking Foot*

## Walking Foot

**Features:**

Griplike teeth on the bottom of a walking foot help feed fabric from the top while your feed dogs feed it from the underside of the fabric. The arm on a walking foot attaches to the needle bar. As the needle moves up and down, the walking foot also moves up and down, walking in harmony with the feed dogs.

**Uses:**

Use a walking foot to keep multiple layers of fabric and batting from shifting as you sew. A walking foot is essential in quilting, but it is also helpful when working with silky fabric, leather, velvet and other hard-to-sew fabrics.

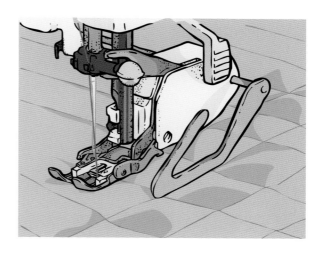

# EDGE-JOINING FOOT

Join the newly formed fan club for this sewing-room superstar! This multipurpose foot is great for joining the edges of small trims and lace, sewing on specialty trim, topstitching and stitching in the ditch as you attach quilt binding.

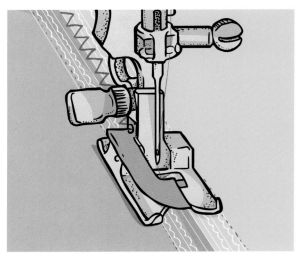

*Edge-Joining Foot*

## Edge-Joining Foot

**Features:**
A sturdy metal edge-joining foot includes a metal guide in front of the center stitch area.

**Uses:**
The metal guide on this foot allows you to easily kiss smaller trims and laces together with precisely aligned edges. Stitches stay perfectly balanced when joining small trims. The metal guide also allows the foot to stitch accurately in the well of a seam as you attach quilt binding.

# PIPING FOOT

Piping is no longer frustrating to sew—this foot makes piping fun to create; plus, you'll enjoy adding beading bling! The channel on this foot's underside allows you to easily add cording, pearls or other dimensional trim to your projects.

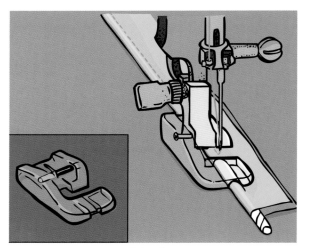

*Piping Foot*

## Piping Foot

**Features:**
A piping foot boasts a hollowed-out channel underneath to help you make or insert piping and add cording to your project in a snap! Use this handy foot with most zigzag sewing machines.

**Uses:**
Create piping using a bias strip and cording with ease. Attach cording or piping along the seam of a garment by creating a piping sandwich and allowing the piping to be guided in the groove of this amazing foot. Adjust your needle position as necessary.

This amazing foot serves a very useful purpose—it keeps fabric edges from rolling as you overcast them. This is especially important if you have ravel-prone edges on your fabric and a serger isn't available. The overcast-guide foot produces functional, pucker-free stitching, keeps the fabric edge flat and finishes raw edges.

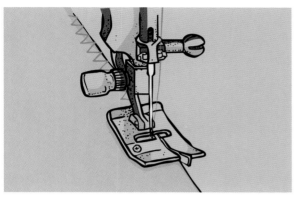

*Overcast-Guide Foot*

## Overcast-Guide Foot

**Features:**

A center bar in the needle opening of an overcast-guide foot keeps the fabric edge flat as you stitch or overcast the edges of your project.

**Uses:**

The overcast-guide foot is designed to produce a smooth, even edge finish, and the center bar prevents the overcast edges from tunneling. Use it with your zigzag stitch and other stitches to overcast seams.

Create delicate pin tucks for heirloom garments or other embellishments. There is no guesswork when you use this amazing grooved foot. The foot is available in several sizes to accommodate your most fanciful projects. Mark the first tuck for accuracy and then guide the remaining tucks in the grooves of the foot for perfectly aligned tucks.

## Pin-Tuck Foot

**Features:**

A pin-tuck foot usually has five, seven or nine parallel grooves on the foot's underside to sew multiple rows of tucks closely and evenly spaced. A pin-tuck foot is made of metal and works in conjunction with a twin needle and a zigzag machine that threads from front to back.

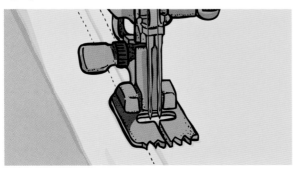

*Pin-Tuck Foot*

**Uses:**

A pin-tuck foot creates small tucks in fabrics such as cotton, linen, silk and taffeta. To achieve a more pronounced pin tuck, use a cord or gimp under the fabric when stitching. The cording and fabric ride in the groove of the pin-tuck foot as you sew. Use a double needle and two threads to sew pin tucks with ease.

### NOTE from NANCY

I have found sizes 5 and 7 to be the most useful pin-tuck feet. Size 9 is used primarily for very small heirloom pintucks.

# FRINGE FOOT

Create dimensional loops on the top surface of fabric with this fanciful foot. Use a fringe foot to make fringe on your project or to employ the thread loops to tack or embellish items.

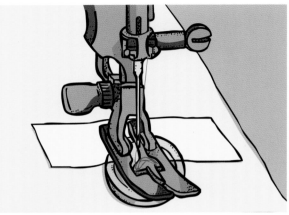

*Fringe Foot*

## Fringe Foot

**Features:**

This metal foot features a raised vertical bar down the center. Stitches form over this bar to create thread loops. Use a zigzag or ladder stitch to create loops. Stitch the loops down and trim the edge to make fringe, or leave them loopy for other applications.

**Uses:**

A versatile fringe foot creates surface texture for embellishing and creating custom trims. Plus, you can use it in garment making. The thread shank created by the center bar is great for sewing on buttons, making bar tacks and attaching shoulder pads.

# MULTICORD FOOT

A multicord foot makes it easy to align several cords or ribbons and couch them in place. The holes in the front of the foot guide three to five cords or decorative threads under the foot and position them for easy stitching. The holes also work well to guide cording through the foot for an easy gathering method. Simply zigzag over the cords and pull them for durable, effortless gathers.

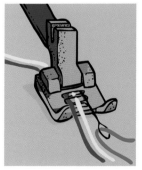 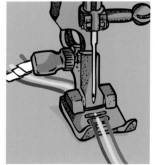

*Multicord Foot*

## Multicord Foot

**Features:**

This metal foot features three to five thread guides for fine cords or decorative thread. The guides keep the cords separated and under control. Each thread feeds through its own hole at the center of the foot and is held under the metal foot during stitching.

## NOTE from NANCY

The serger looper threader on page 73 works well to thread cording through the holes in the multicord foot. Tape each threaded cord to the base of the machine with removable tape. This will prevent them from pulling out as the remaining cords are threaded. After all cords are threaded, knot them together to keep them from slipping out.

**Uses:**

A multicord foot holds cords neatly in place as you zigzag (couch) them in place. A multicord foot is ideal for adding decorative thread or embroidery floss. You can easily couch cording with matching, contrasting or clear thread in the needle. Stitch slowly to keep the cording or ribbons flat. The foot may also be used for gathering.

Lots of ruffles to make? No problem! Use a handy ruffler foot to create yards and yards of evenly spaced ruffles or pleats. This foot works best on a lower-line to midline machine rather than on a computerized machine. Although the foot looks rather scary, it works like a dream! Take time to put a ruffler foot on your machine correctly and make a test ruffle. You'll love the amount of time you save over conventional ruffling methods!

## Ruffler Foot

### Features:

This large metal foot has a lever to adjust the fullness of gathers or pleats. The pleat fullness lever has three to four settings. There is also a pleat-depth screw. Place your fabric under the separator guide between the ruffling blade and the separator blades for normal gathering. By changing the way the fabric is placed in the guide and blades, you can attach ruffles as you sew them.

### Uses:

A ruffler foot is perfect for making dust ruffles, curtain ruffles, ruffled garments and pillows with ruffles. You'll love the convenience of being able to gather or pleat a ruffle and attach it to your project in one easy step. How cool is that?

*Ruffler Foot*

## NOTE from NANCY

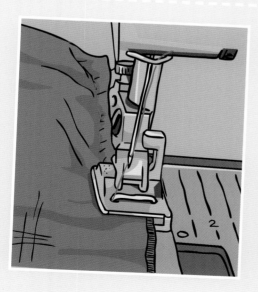

Don't confuse a ruffler foot with a gathering foot. A gathering foot is used mainly with lightweight fabrics, while a ruffler foot can be used on many different fabrics. You can set the pleat fullness lever on a ruffler foot so that it gathers every stitch, every sixth stitch, every twelfth stitch or not at all. This allows you to gather certain areas and simply flip the lever to leave other areas flat with no gathers. There is no need to change the foot back to a regular foot for straight stitching. A gathering foot gathers basically in a 2:1 ratio, depending on the fabric, and you may tighten the gathering by pulling the bobbin thread. A gathering foot works well for small areas, but if you are working on a dust ruffle, curtains or another large project, you will most definitely want to use a ruffler foot!

# A SEWING BUDDY

When I first had the "notion" to start sewing, I joined 4-H. I knew sewing was something I wanted to do, and yet I wanted to have some company. I am so glad I did, because when you have someone to share your accomplishments with, it is so much more rewarding. Plus, those projects that don't turn out quite as you hoped don't seem so catastrophic when there is someone else saying, "Oh, that happened to me the first time I tried it, too."

I have always kept a Sewing Buddy at my side over the years. My notion's business, Nancy's Notions, has allowed me to confide with over 150 Sewing Buddies, and my television show provides many, many more.

Choose a friend to share your passion, whether it's quilting, embroidery, serging, felting, sewing or crafting. If you are too shy or too busy for a huggable buddy, choose an online friend, or blog with other people who share your enthusiasm. Enjoy a rich and rewarding sewing experience!

*Nancy Zieman*

### Natalie Sewell & Nancy

*Natalie and Nancy plan at least quarterly quilting dates, always meeting in Natalie's Studio in Madison, Wisconsin, to work on landscape quilt projects and solve the world's problems!*

### Natalie & Nancy Teaching Together

*Natalie Sewell and Nancy presenting a seminar, showing off Natalie's Quilt, Grey Day in August.*

## Eileen Roche & Nancy

*Embroidery is the topic
when Nancy plans
a sewing date with Eileen.*

## Donna Fenske & Nancy

*Nancy and Donna have been sewing together
in preparation for Sewing With Nancy
since 1984. In the early years, they sewed
together in a basement sewing room!*

## Mary Mulari & Nancy

*Mary has earned the title as
Sewing With Nancy's Most Frequent Guest!
For the past six years, the two sewing
buddies plan a weekend of sewing
in Mary's Studio in Aurora, Minnesota.*

¼" Quilting Foot . . . . . . . . . . . . . . . . . . . . . . 115

1" × 6" Ruler . . . . . . . . . . . . . . . . . . . . . . . . . . 20

12-in-1 Multi Tool . . . . . . . . . . . . . . . . . . . . 15

5-in-1 Tool . . . . . . . . . . . . . . . . . . . . . . 20, 55

6" Seam Gauge . . . . . . . . . . . . . . . . . . . . . . 20

Add-A-Quarter . . . . . . . . . . . . . . . . . . . . . . 54

Adhesive Quilting Guide . . . . . . . . . . . . . 12

Adjustable Rulers . . . . . . . . . . . . . . . . . . . . 46

Air-Erasable Pen . . . . . . . . . . . . . . . . . . . . . 8

Appliqué Pins . . . . . . . . . . . . . . . . . . . . . . . 16

Appliqué Pressing Sheet . . . . . . . . . . . . . 88

Appliqué Scissors . . . . . . . . . . . . . . . . . . . 27

Automatic Needle Threader . . . . . . . . . . 23

Awl . . . . . . . . . . . . . . . . . . . . . . . . . . . . . . . . 28

Bags, travel . . . . . . . . . . . . . . . . . . . . . . . . . 41

Ballpoint Pins . . . . . . . . . . . . . . . . . . . . . . 17

Ballpoint Bodkin . . . . . . . . . . . . . . . . . . . . 96

Basic Notions . . . . . . . . . . . . . . . . . . . . 8-29

Bendable Bright Light . . . . . . . . . . . . . . . 33

Bias Tape Makers . . . . . . . . . . . . . . . . . . . 94

Big Foot . . . . . . . . . . . . . . . . . . . . . . . . . . 116

Binding Tools . . . . . . . . . . . . . . . . . . . . . . 56

Binding Clips . . . . . . . . . . . . . . . . . . . . . . . 56

Binding Buddy Ruler . . . . . . . . . . . . . . . . 56

Block Markers . . . . . . . . . . . . . . . . . . . . . . 52

Blunt Serrated-Edge Tracing Wheel . . . . . . 10

Blunt Smooth-Edge Tracing Wheel . . . . . . 10

Bob 'n Serge . . . . . . . . . . . . . . . . . . . . . . . 76

Bobbin Organizers . . . . . . . . . . . . . . . . . . 37

Bobbin Side Winder . . . . . . . . . . . . . . . . . 99

Bobbin and Spool Organizer . . . . . . . . . 37

Bobbin Tower . . . . . . . . . . . . . . . . . . . . . . 37

Bodkin . . . . . . . . . . . . . . . . . . . . . . . . . 29, 96

Buttonhole Cutters . . . . . . . . . . . . . . . . . . 18

Buttonhole Scissors . . . . . . . . . . . . . . . . . 18

Canned Air . . . . . . . . . . . . . . . . . . . . . . . . . 80

Canvas Weights . . . . . . . . . . . . . . . . . . . . . 13

Chalk . . . . . . . . . . . . . . . . . . . . . . . . . . . . . . . 9

Chalk Liner . . . . . . . . . . . . . . . . . . . . . . . . . . 9

Chenille Cutters . . . . . . . . . . . . . . . . . . . . 99

Chisel and Mat . . . . . . . . . . . . . . . . . . . . . 18

Circle Cutting Aids . . . . . . . . . . . . . . . . . . 55

Circle Weights . . . . . . . . . . . . . . . . . . . . . . 13

Circle Template . . . . . . . . . . . . . . . . . . . . . 55

Clapper . . . . . . . . . . . . . . . . . . . . . . . . . . . . 89

Clear Rulers . . . . . . . . . . . . . . . . . . . . . . . . 46

Clearly Perfect Angles . . . . . . . . . . . . . . . 50

Curved Embroidery Scissors . . . . . . . . . . 64

Cutter Glide . . . . . . . . . . . . . . . . . . . . . . . . 45

Cutting Mats . . . . . . . . . . . . . . . . . . . . 48-49

Design Walls . . . . . . . . . . . . . . . . . . . . . . . 53

Diamond-Shaped Needle Threader . . . . . 22

Dome Threaded Needle Case . . . . . . . . . 68

Dressmaker Pins . . . . . . . . . . . . . . . . . . . . 16

Dressmaker's Shears . . . . . . . . . . . . . . . . . 26

Easy Angle . . . . . . . . . . . . . . . . . . . . . . . . . 50

Edge-Joining Foot . . . . . . . . . . . . . . . . . . 118

Embroidery Bag . . . . . . . . . . . . . . . . . . . . 41

Embroidery Clippers . . . . . . . . . . . . . . . . 64

Ergonomic Seam Ripper . . . . . . . . . . . . . 15

EZ Tool Cleaner and Cutter Glide . . . . . . . 45

Fabric Pincushion . . . . . . . . . . . . . . . . . . . 14

Fabric Press Cloth . . . . . . . . . . . . . . . . . . . 88

Fabric Storage . . . . . . . . . . . . . . . . . . . . . . 34

Fashion Design Kit . . . . . . . . . . . . . . . . . . . . . .107

Fasturn Set . . . . . . . . . . . . . . . . . . . . . . . . . . . . .105

Fat-Quarter Bags . . . . . . . . . . . . . . . . . . . . . . . .34

Fat-Quarter Boxes . . . . . . . . . . . . . . . . . . . . . . .34

Fat-Quarter Cards and Bands . . . . . . . . . . . .35

Felting Tools . . . . . . . . . . . . . . . . . . . . . . . . . . . .69

Flat-Head Pins . . . . . . . . . . . . . . . . . . . . . . . . . .16

Flexible Bodkins . . . . . . . . . . . . . . . . . . . . . . . .96

Flexible Ruler . . . . . . . . . . . . . . . . . . . . . . . . . .106

Flip-n-Set Tool . . . . . . . . . . . . . . . . . . . . . . . . . .51

Floor Lamp . . . . . . . . . . . . . . . . . . . . . . . . . . . . .32

Fluorescent Tape . . . . . . . . . . . . . . . . . . . . . . . .47

Foam Bobbin Box . . . . . . . . . . . . . . . . . . . . . . .37

Free-Motion Quilting Foot . . . . . . . . . . . . . .116

French Curve Ruler . . . . . . . . . . . . . . . . . . . . .107

Fringe Foot . . . . . . . . . . . . . . . . . . . . . . . . . . . .120

Get Squared Ruler . . . . . . . . . . . . . . . . . . . . . .52

Glass-Head Silk Pins . . . . . . . . . . . . . . . . . . . .17

Grasshopper Scissors . . . . . . . . . . . . . . . . . . .65

Gypsy Gripper . . . . . . . . . . . . . . . . . . . . . . . . .48

Half-Square Triangle Helpers . . . . . . . . . . .50-51

Hand Needle Felting Tools . . . . . . . . . . . . . .69

Handsewing Needle Threaders . . . . . . . . . .22

Hem Clips . . . . . . . . . . . . . . . . . . . . . . . . . . . . .56

Hem Gauge . . . . . . . . . . . . . . . . . . . . . . . . . . .109

Hem Markers . . . . . . . . . . . . . . . . . . . . . . . . .108

Hot-Fix Applicator Wand . . . . . . . . . . . . . . .103

Irons . . . . . . . . . . . . . . . . . . . . . . . . . . . . . . .84-85

Ironing Boards . . . . . . . . . . . . . . . . . . . . . .86-87

Ironing Spray . . . . . . . . . . . . . . . . . . . . . . . . . .87

Kwik Klip . . . . . . . . . . . . . . . . . . . . . . . . . . . . . .57

Lamps . . . . . . . . . . . . . . . . . . . . . . . . . . . . . . . .32

Leather Thimble . . . . . . . . . . . . . . . . . . . . . . .19

Lickity Grip . . . . . . . . . . . . . . . . . . . . . . . . . . . .58

Light Box . . . . . . . . . . . . . . . . . . . . . . . . . . . . .100

Lighted Seam Ripper . . . . . . . . . . . . . . . . . . .15

Lighting . . . . . . . . . . . . . . . . . . . . . . . . . . . .32, 33

Little Foot . . . . . . . . . . . . . . . . . . . . . . . . . . . .115

Locking Tweezers . . . . . . . . . . . . . . . . . . . . . .72

Loop Turner . . . . . . . . . . . . . . . . . . . . . . . . . .104

Looper Threader . . . . . . . . . . . . . . . . . . . . . . .73

Machine-Needle Inserter/Threader . . . . . . .24

Magnetic Needle Case . . . . . . . . . . . . . . . . . .69

Magnetic Pincushion . . . . . . . . . . . . . . . . . . .14

Magnetic Seam Guide . . . . . . . . . . . . . . . . . .12

Magnifying Tweezers . . . . . . . . . . . . . . . . . . .72

Marking Pens . . . . . . . . . . . . . . . . . . . . . . . . . .8

Marking Tape for Rulers . . . . . . . . . . . . . . . .47

Microserrated-Edge Shears . . . . . . . . . . . . . .26

Mini Irons . . . . . . . . . . . . . . . . . . . . . . . . . . . . .85

Mini Measurement Gauge . . . . . . . . . . . . . . .20

Mini Vacuum Attachments . . . . . . . . . . . .33, 81

Multicord Foot . . . . . . . . . . . . . . . . . . . . . . . .120

Needle Cases . . . . . . . . . . . . . . . . . . . . . . . .68-69

Needle Gripper . . . . . . . . . . . . . . . . . . . . . . . .25

Needle-Gripping Tools . . . . . . . . . . . . . . . . . .25

Needle Holders . . . . . . . . . . . . . . . . . . . . . . . .68

Needle Inserter and Threader . . . . . . . . . . . .24

Needle Threader, Hand . . . . . . . . . . . . . . .22-23

Needle Threader, Machine . . . . . . . . . . . . . . .24

Needlepoint Tracing Wheel . . . . . . . . . . . . . .10

Needle Puller . . . . . . . . . . . . . . . . . . . . . . . . . .25

Needle Sharpeners . . . . . . . . . . . . . . . . . . . .110

Neez-ez . . . . . . . . . . . . . . . . . . . . . . . . . . . . . . .79

No-Math Miter . . . . . . . . . . . . . . . . . . . . . . . .101

Notions Bag . . . . . . . . . . . . . . . . . . . . . . . . . . .41

On-Point Triangle Tool.....................51

Open-Toe Foot..........................114

Organizational Tools.....................31-41

Original Big Board........................86

Overcast-Guide Foot.....................119

Padded Pressing Notions.................90

Painter's Tape............................47

Pattern Boxes............................38

Pattern Keepers..........................38

Pattern Notcher..........................98

Pattern Organizers.......................38

Pattern Weights..........................13

Pebble Needle Case......................68

Pedal-Sta II..............................79

Pens, marking.............................8

Peggy's Stitch Eraser.....................66

Pins....................................16-17

Pincher-Type Bodkins....................96

Pincushions...............................14

Pinking Shears...........................26

Pin-tuck Foot............................119

Piping Foot..............................118

Pocket Template.........................95

Point Presser and Clapper................89

Portable Design Wall.....................53

Portable Pressing Mats...................87

Press/Cut Mat...........................49

Pressing Bars...........................111

Pressing Boards.........................89

Pressing Tools..........................82-91

Pressing Ham............................90

Pressing Surfaces........................86

Professional Iron.........................84

Quarter-Inch Marking Tools...............54

Quick Quarter............................51

Quilt Clips...............................57

Quilt Halo................................59

Quilt Layering Tools......................57

Quilt Pounce.............................54

Quilting Notions.........................42-59

Quilter's Tote.............................41

Quilting Gloves..........................58

Quilting Pins.............................16

Retractable Tape Measure................21

Reverse-action Tweezers.................72

Rotary Cutter Blade Sharpener............45

Rotary-Blade Care Products..............45

Rotary Circle Cutter.....................55

Rotary Cutters...........................44

Rotary Cutting Mats.....................48-49

Ruffler Foot.............................121

Rulers............................46, 56, 106-107

Ruler Gripper Handles....................48

Ruler, Mat and Tool Organizer.............36

Ruler Storage.............................36

Safety Pins.............................29, 57

Safety-Pin Covers........................57

Scissors...............................27, 64-65

Scrap Catcher...........................78

Seam Gauges............................20

Seam Rippers..........................15, 77

Seam Ripper Clipper...................15, 77

Seam Rolls.............................90-91

Seam Sealants...........................75

Seam Stick...............................89

Serger Brush.............................81

Serger Foot Pads . . . . . . . . . . . . . . . . . . . . . .79

Serger Looper Threader . . . . . . . . . . . . . . . .73

Serger Notions . . . . . . . . . . . . . . . . . . . . . .70-81

Serger Seam Rippers . . . . . . . . . . . . . . . . . . .77

Serger Trolley. . . . . . . . . . . . . . . . . . . . . . . . .40

Serger Tweezers . . . . . . . . . . . . . . . . . . . . . . .72

Serger Upkeep Tools . . . . . . . . . . . . . . . . .80-81

Sew Easy Guide Set . . . . . . . . . . . . . . . . . . .50

Sewing Buddy . . . . . . . . . . . . . . . . . . . .122-123

Sewing-Machine Feet . . . . . . . . . . . . . . .112-121

Sewing-Machine Seam Guides . . . . . . . . . .12

Sewing-Machine Trolley . . . . . . . . . . . . . . .40

Shaped Weights. . . . . . . . . . . . . . . . . . . . . .13

Shears . . . . . . . . . . . . . . . . . . . . . . . . . . . . . .26

SimFlex Expanding Gauge. . . . . . . . . . . . . .97

Sixth Finger Stiletto . . . . . . . . . . . . . . . . . .28

Spiral Eye Needle. . . . . . . . . . . . . . . . . . . . .23

Spool Adaptor . . . . . . . . . . . . . . . . . . . . . . .62

Spring-Action Nippers. . . . . . . . . . . . . . . . .65

Spring-Action Scissors. . . . . . . . . . . . . . . . .27

Standard Tape Measure . . . . . . . . . . . . . . . .21

Standard Thimble . . . . . . . . . . . . . . . . . . . .19

Starch Alternative . . . . . . . . . . . . . . . . . . . .87

Steam Generator . . . . . . . . . . . . . . . . . . . . .84

Stencil Marking Tools. . . . . . . . . . . . . . . . . .54

Stilettos . . . . . . . . . . . . . . . . . . . . . . . . . . . .28

Supreme Slider. . . . . . . . . . . . . . . . . . . . . . .59

Surgical Seam Ripper. . . . . . . . . . . . . . . . . .77

Tabletop Ironing Board. . . . . . . . . . . . . . . .86

Tabletop Lamp . . . . . . . . . . . . . . . . . . . . . . .32

Tabletop/Hanging Ruler Holder . . . . . . . . .36

Tabletop Thread Racks. . . . . . . . . . . . . . . . .39

Tailor Board . . . . . . . . . . . . . . . . . . . . . . . . .89

Tailor's Chalk . . . . . . . . . . . . . . . . . . . . . . . . .9

Tape Measures . . . . . . . . . . . . . . . . . . . . . . .21

Task Lighting. . . . . . . . . . . . . . . . . . . . . .32, 33

Telescoping Extension Magnet . . . . . . . . . .102

Thimbles. . . . . . . . . . . . . . . . . . . . . . . . . . . .19

Thread Tools . . . . . . . . . . . . . . . . . . . . . .60-69

Thread Braid . . . . . . . . . . . . . . . . . . . . . . . . .67

Thread Conditioner . . . . . . . . . . . . . . . . . . .64

Thread Guides . . . . . . . . . . . . . . . . . . . . . . .62

Thread Heaven. . . . . . . . . . . . . . . . . . . . . . .64

Thread Nets . . . . . . . . . . . . . . . . . . . . . . . . .74

Thread Organizers. . . . . . . . . . . . . . . . . .39, 63

Thread Remover . . . . . . . . . . . . . . . . . . . . .66

Thread Stands. . . . . . . . . . . . . . . . . . . . .39, 63

Threader and Tweezer Bodkin . . . . . . . . . . .29

Totes. . . . . . . . . . . . . . . . . . . . . . . . . . . . . . .41

Tracing Paper . . . . . . . . . . . . . . . . . . . . . . . .11

Tracing Wheels. . . . . . . . . . . . . . . . . . . . . . .10

Trolleys. . . . . . . . . . . . . . . . . . . . . . . . . . . . .40

Trolley Needle. . . . . . . . . . . . . . . . . . . . . . . .28

Tube Turners . . . . . . . . . . . . . . . . . . . . .104-105

Turnable Mats. . . . . . . . . . . . . . . . . . . . . . . .49

Tweezers. . . . . . . . . . . . . . . . . . . . . . . . . . . .72

Two-Needle Installer . . . . . . . . . . . . . . . . . .24

Vacuum Attachments . . . . . . . . . . . . . . .33, 81

Walking Foot. . . . . . . . . . . . . . . . . . . . . . . .117

Wall Thread Racks . . . . . . . . . . . . . . . . . . . .39

Water-Erasable Pen. . . . . . . . . . . . . . . . . . . . .8

White Marking Pen. . . . . . . . . . . . . . . . . . . . .8

Wide Bodkin . . . . . . . . . . . . . . . . . . . . . . . . .29

Wonder Thread Guide. . . . . . . . . . . . . . . . . .62

Wooden Wedge Iron . . . . . . . . . . . . . . . . . .85

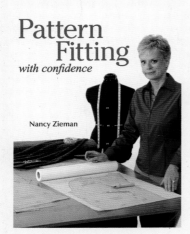